A JOURNAL OF
CONSCIOUSNESS AND TRANSFORMATION

ReVision

CONTENTS

Dreaming at the Edges
Helena Daly and Karen Jaenke, Editors

1 Editor's Introduction: Dreaming at the Edges
   Helena Daly & Karen Jaenke

5 Dreaming with the Collective: Invitation to Interiority
   Karen Jaenke, PhD

9 Hypnopompic Encounter: Death's Shadow and Light Between the Realms
   Helena Daly, PhD

25 Poem: The Quest
   Meredith Sabini, PhD

27 Expansion and Contraction in the Dreaming Body
   Karen Jaenke, PhD

41 Heart-Knowing, Somatic Dreaming, and Transsubjectivity:
   A Scholarly Personal Narrative
   Daniel Deslauriers, PhD

49 Poem: Boundaries
   Meredith Sabini, PhD

Cover photo by Karen Jaenke
Winter 2022 • Volume 34 • Number 1

What Is ReVision?

Revisioning, as the name ReVision hints, has been central to the publication's forty year historical trajectory. As our understanding of the leading edge of transformative and consciousness-changing thinking has developed, so has the focus of our mission.

From its origins in humanistic and transpersonal psychologies, ReVision has shifted toward a framework of transdisciplinary, decolonial, and indigenous paradigms. From its origins as an academic journal it has shifted toward a publication which includes art, poetry, story, and articles that translate topics for a broader audience.

With a commitment to the future of humanity and all our relations, ReVision is dedicated to the exploration of issues that assert and value the transmotional and interconnected sovereignty of people before any institutions. Sovereignty and self-determination as foundations of peace require our human imagination as part of a sustainable world of stories and cultural practices in a particular place or ecology.

ReVision welcomes submissions from a wide range of disciplines using a broad spectrum of formats to deepen the process of inquiry, dialogue, and engaged participatory knowing and conversation.

Karen Jaenke

Volume 34, Number 1 (ISBN 978-1-7362314-1-8)

ReVision (ISSN 0275-6935) is published by
The Society for Indigenous and Ancestral Wisdom and Healing.

Copyright © 2024 ReVision Publishing.
Copyright retained by author when noted. The views expressed are not necessarily those of ReVision or its editors.

ReVision provides opportunities for publishing divergent opinions, ideas, or judgments.

Manuscript Submissions

We welcome manuscript submissions. Manuscript guidelines can be found on our webpage: http://revisionpublishing.org.

POSTMASTER: Send address changes to
ReVision Publishing,
P.O. Box 1855,
Sebastopol, CA 95473.

Subscriptions

For subscriptions mail a check to above address or go to www.revisionpublishing.org.

Individual Subscriptions

Subscription for one year: $36 online only,
$36 print only (international $72),
$48 print and on-line (international $84).

Subscription for two years: $60 online only,
$60 print only (international $96),
$79 print and online (international $115).

Subscription for three years: $72 online only,
$72 print only (international $108),
$96 print and online (international $132).

Institutional Subscriptions

$98 online only (international $134),
$134 print and online (international $191).

Please allow six weeks for delivery of first issue.

Editorial Board

Editor
Jürgen Werner Kremer
Santa Rosa Junior College, Santa Rosa, CA

Associate Editor
Karen Jaenke, PhD
Independent Scholar, Richmond, CA

Editorial and Production Management Team

Cristina Kaplan, MA	Gary Newman	Samuel A. Malkemus, PhD
Poetry Editor	Design and Production	Book Review Editor

Consulting Editors

John Adams, PhD
Saybrook University, San Francisco, CA

Matthew C. Bronson, PhD
O'Reilly School of Technology, UC Davis, Davis, CA

Allan Combs, PhD
California Institute of Integral Studies, San Francisco, CA

Apela Colorado, PhD
Worldwide Indigenous Science Network

Jorge Ferrer, PhD
California Institute of Integral Studies, San Francisco, CA

Mary Gomes, PhD
Sonoma State University, Rohnert Park, CA

Stanislav Grof, MD
California Institute of Integral Studies, San Francisco, CA

Stanley Krippner, PhD
Saybrook University, San Francisco, CA

Joan Marler, MA
California Institute of Integral Studies, San Francisco, CA

S. Lily Mendoza, PhD
Oakland University, Rochester, MI

Alfonso Montuori, PhD
California Institute of Integral Studies, San Francisco, CA

Glenn Aparicio Parry, PhD
Circle for Original Thinking, Albuquerque, NM

James W. Perkinson, PhD
Ecumenical Theological Seminary, Detroit, MI

Joseph Prabhu, PhD
California State University Los Angeles, CA

Donald Rothberg, PhD
Spirit Rock Meditation Center, Woodacre, CA

Meredith Sabini, PhD
The Dream Institute of Northern California, Berkeley, CA

Elenita Strobel, EdD
Sonoma State University, Rohnert Park, CA

ReVision Abstracts

Vol. 34 No. 1 • Winter 2023

Daly, H., Hypnopompic Encounter: Death's Shadow and Light Between the Realms. *ReVision, 34(1)*, 13-23. doi:10.4298/REVN.34.1.00-00

The dream-waking state (the hypnopompic state of consciousness) that opens between sleeping and waking realms is an important state of consciousness, yet largely forgotten, overlooked and misunderstood. The hypnopompic state is rarely differentiated from the hypnagogic state—the state of consciousness that opens at the other end of the spectrum, prior to falling asleep, yet crucial and significant differences do exist. This article details the differences, illustrating them with an extraordinary, personal hypnopompic encounter, and ancient knowledge, depth psychological and transpersonal perspectives. Doing so, will highlight the dream-waking state as a third state of being—a liminal state through which higher states of awareness, embodied knowledge, healing, and the workings of soul and its relation to death and beyond can be known and experienced.

Deslauriers, D., Heart-Knowing, Somatic Dreaming, and Transsubjectivity: A Scholarly Personal Narrative. *ReVision, 34(1)*, 13-23. doi:10.4298/REVN.34.1.00-00

A narrative inquiry, triggered by a hypnopompic dream, unfolds the social-somatic reality of heart knowing. This inquiry discloses a complex relational topography within which childhood memories, therapeutic encounter, existential issues around elder care and somatic relational-knowing co-mingle within the dream meaning-making process. Dreams' concerns being at their core relational, it is suggested that intersubjectivity is pervasive, and perhaps primary, in meaning-making. In turn, dream insights can infuse and inform a relationship's course. Opening the question of what informs the experience of heart knowing, the notion of transsubjectivity is explored. The latter is viewed as an incipient, yet patterning, knowing field.

Jaenke, K., Dreaming with the Collective: Invitation to Interiority. *ReVision, 34(1)*, 00-00. doi:10.4298/REVN.34.1.00-00

This column examines a dream that highlights interiority as a defining feature of the sacred feminine. The central dream image—a numinous box, containing a series of nested boxes, similar to the Russian dolls—emphasizes receding degrees of hiddenness, interiority, depth and subtlety. While the interior-exterior distinction mirrors female and male genitalia, more fundamentally it denotes two prime ways of orienting and organizing human consciousness, two alternative approaches to life. The exterior orientation of patriarchal societies predisposes us to extract all meaning, purpose and value from the external world. Collective loss of access to the richness of an interior universe of depth, afflicting both society and planet, finds correction in a fundamental shift in orientation from exterior to interior.

Jaenke, K., Expansion and Contraction in the Dreaming Body. *ReVision, 34(1)*, 00-00. doi:10.4298/REVN.34.1.00-00

Dreams amplify dynamics of expansion and contraction in the body, which can be beneficially engaged during hypnopompia to resolve the constrictions of trauma and open to the expansiveness of joy. Gendlin's focusing method (of attending to the felt sense as a guide to growth directions and leading to expansive possibilities) is applied to several of the author's extraordinary dreams. The somatic-energetic stirrings of dreams are revealed as encompassing the full continuum of expansion and contraction, akin to the cosmos itself. Consciously engaging states of contraction awakened by dreams resolves trauma's residue in the energy body, while shifting contraction towards spaciousness and joy. Mindfully participating in the somatic dynamics of expansion and contraction conveys felt participation in the elemental dynamics of the universe.

Editor's Introduction

Dreaming at the Edges

Helena Daly, PhD

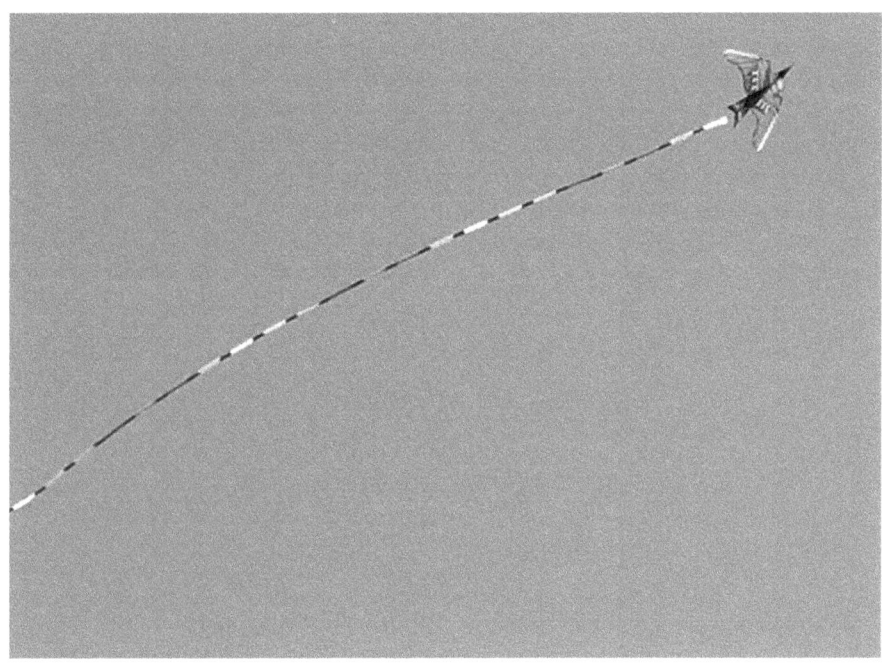

Photo: Flying Free, Karen Jaenke

W.B. Yeats, whose trust in sleep and dream was well known, once remarked "all that I know of any value has come from sleep" (Bridge, 1953, p. 147). The authors in this issue share this perspective, showing that some of our most profound transformative experiences occur during sleep in deep dream states, and in liminal moments upon awakening between the worlds. The mysterious subtle presence encountered within the spatial depth of sleeping and dreaming led the Irish visionary George Russell (A.E) to wonder, if perhaps "the black curtain of unconsciousness which drapes the chambers of the brain, is lifted, granting, if for an instant, a glimpse of the high adventures of the sleeping soul" (A.E. 1918, p. 79).

William James (2005) wondered if the visible waking state might be but one special type of consciousness, "parted by the filmiest of screens behind which lie potential forms of consciousness, entirely different" (p. 155). These other forms of subtle consciousness James described as subliminal doors through which divine impressions are made. One condition under which this unveiling takes place lies deep within sleep and dream and upon awakening wherein sleeping, dreaming and waking realms overlap. This intermediary spatial domain between the worlds is referred to in academic circles as the hypnopompic state of consciousness—a special focus of the articles in this issue.

From within the depths of our being, during sleeping, dreaming and waking, the mysteries and passages of what lie beneath, between and beyond are revealed. For we are as Martin Heidegger beautifully says, "custodians of deep and ancient thresholds" (as cited in O' Donahue, 1998, p. 42). Threshold experiences are revealed from within the spatial dimensionality that opens in sleeping-dreaming domains. From within these depths and in those liminal moments upon awakening, subtle revelatory experiences unfold through which perceptual alterations and spiritual transmissions are received. When the depths of

---

Helena Daly, PhD works as a *Spiritual Care Provider* at the University of California San Francisco, Parnassus Campus (UCSF). Before recently returning to the US, she worked as a *Spiritual and Psychological Care Practitioner* in Hospice and Palliative Care in Ireland. Helena holds a special interest in end-of-life phenomenal experiences (dreams, visions and death-bed encounters) and is currently writing her first book which is full of stories about extraordinary dreaming and waking experiences in relation to death and beyond. She holds a PhD in East-West Psychology with a specialization in dreams and hypnopompic consciousness. Previous qualifications include: MA in Counseling, BA in Psychology and RGN when working in London. She can be contacted at helenacdaly@gmail.com or through her website www.helenadalyphd.com.

consciousness are inwardly opened, living manifestations of soul, of ancient presence, deep heart knowing and remembrance are known and experienced, uncovering the spiritual potentialities of human life.

Heidegger (1926) speaks to these potentialities/possibilities as 'ontological priority.' The importance of dream life is reflected upon throughout the following articles, grounded in personal accounts of transpersonal dreaming and waking encounters. These articles offer descriptive illustrations of emerging subtle consciousness—raw perceptual transmissions that show dreaming as a revelatory ground that can and does reveal profound ontological depth. And when the ontological ground of being is reflexively engaged and participated in, meaning and significance is disclosed. This dynamic process of unfolding perception highlights dreams and dream-waking states of being as powerful innate epistemological sources of knowledge through which fundamental insight into life can be made.

1957/1983, p. 10). For it is subtle consciousness—potential and actual forms of subtle life that come through our inner world, through the peripheries of life, and in the in-between spaces, that give rise to profound, transformative shifts in consciousness with life-changing outcomes. In dreams—home to the wanderings of subtle life itself—the constricted waking egoic self undergoes radical deconstruction and re-formation.

As human beings, we are innately endowed with the gift of dreaming—regularly occurring subtle phenomenon that are an intrinsic part of the human condition. Dreams, live creative expressions of the psyche, known and experienced from the inside-out, are less subject to the harsh deadening effect of too much reason, rationality and endless caution—those domineering elements of the intellect so intrinsic to western concepts of consciousness.

Dreams, free from social censure, are altered states that unfold within the transformed, subtle domain of sleep. When

of inner life. Metaphysical teachings from the ancient world along with indigenous perspectives are founded upon disciplined engagement with rigorous internal experiences, such as those documented by contemplatives, mystics, shamans and medicine people, as distinct from the outer external orientation of the modern scientist (Progroff, 1957/1983).

In bringing forth embodied perceptual transmissions received in sleep, and metaphysical revelations that open through a process-oriented unfolding deep within the body, somatic correlates of psychic events that manifest within primitive layers of psyche are highlighted. Within the altered state of dreams, psychic and somatic counterparts dynamically interact, offering metaphysical revelations that transcend older dualistic conceptions that split psyche and soma. Hypnopompic openings, in particular, help close the gap between soma and psyche by bringing forth implicit experiential knowing of psychosomatic processes. Attending to subtle consciousness, with its energetic unfolding, offers refined discriminations within the mind-body-spirit-soul continuum.

The body serves as the medium for the expression and realization of being. It is through the body that inner life is accessed, and non-ordinary/transpersonal and higher cosmic perceptions explored and known (Irwin, 2015, p. 14). Thus, bringing forth the fruits of embodied, subtle life, is "crucial for the actualization of deep consciousness potential" (Irwin, 2015, p. 18), and central to the self's unfolding and development.

> *In dreams—home to the wanderings of subtle life itself—the constricted waking egoic self undergoes radical deconstruction and re-formation.*

The actualizing potential released through these types of visionary experiences carries a bodily and energetic component, with deep bodily resonances—undeniable inner energetics that serve as guiding intuitions in the outer waking world—the field of incarnation through which the actualizing process unfolds. These subtle experiences, awakened through dreams, generate a positive impact on human growth for the engaged recipient.

Our bodies—our homes, through which we experience inner and outer life, are so often left out in intellectual pursuits and transpersonal thought and inquiry, and yet the body is the channel through which all perceptual unfolding emerges, develops, deepens, integrates, and transforms.

Dreaming at the Edges addresses a deficit in psychology, a science still stifled "by the fact that it has not been able to deal scientifically with subtle consciousness" (Progroff,

dropping down into the dark dead of night, naturally occurring liminal conditions are crossed, granting easy exploration of transpersonal phenomena. The study of dreams, as a regular and naturally-occurring altered state of consciousness, can greatly advance and expand our understanding of the self and the field of psychology.

Throughout this dream issue, each author, in their own unique way, shows how vitally important it is that methods of inquiry be led from the inside-out, through deep experiential knowing. These articles also highlight how embodied dream knowledge significantly informs depth psychological, transpersonal and archetypal theories and concepts, frameworks and worldviews. Yet well before the advent of depth psychology in the 20th century, significant introspective, experiential work emerged in the understanding and channeling of subtle dynamic processes

Dream research rooted in embodied knowledge, therefore, holds enormous potential in helping bridge the great divide within the scientific study of consciousness that sits between materialistic and nonmaterialistic views of the mind. Higher states of awareness, accessed and explored by dream practitioners, continually show that direct subjective experience is a profound and rich qualitative resource in consciousness and psychology research that can expand and enrich our understanding of the far edges of the human self.

It is vitally important and necessary then, to create and develop approaches and embodied methods of inquiry within dream research that carry interpretive value—working models that help highlight and explore the meaningful significance transformative dreaming and waking experiences hold. Approaching dreams as revelatory phenomena, and the hypnopompic realm as a revelatory state, provides a fresh new way of seeing and perceiving. Embracing the hypnopompic realm as an energetically emerging third mode or being, or post-dual third that sits in the middle—within continual, dynamic interaction between psyche and soma, allows for the bridging and synthesis of apparently separate domains of experience.

This open approach is in line with current concepts of consciousness that take into account reflexivity inherent in whole experience that cannot be split or reduced.

Engaging consciously with extreme states as an approach demonstrates a coming into being not through abstract reasoning alone but through a deeply embodied practice. This natural way of working opens into complex, generative states of inner, in-between and outer reality, disclosing transpersonal depths of interiority associated with archetypal structures and visions. Multiple forms of subtle consciousness help balance and revise more rational, materialistic, and externally-oriented scientific perspectives, that have dominated how we in the modern West make sense of reality.

This approach brings the dreamer's critical, reflexive and observational awareness to bear upon the embodied and subtle states of being that are dramatically altered through dreaming and non-ordinary consciousness. Deep, reflective experiencing of transpersonal states, along with rich documented descriptions of unfolding subtle phenomena, contribute to the development of a science of subjectivity. Building from the experiential ground of naturally occurring altered dreaming and waking states, deep psychological exploration and critical reflective methods of analysis contribute to an enriched and expanded understanding of the subtle complexities and edges of the self.

This special issue on "Dreaming at the Edges" offers a small but significant step in that direction, thus contributing to the field of transpersonal dream research and practice—and expanded visions of human selfhood.

Overview of Articles

The articles in this issue adopt scholarly personal narrative, offering innovative approaches and creative, transpersonal methods of inquiry to the exploration, reflection and discussion of deep dreaming and waking encounters.

This issue introduces a new column entitled "Dreaming with the Collective," which will address cultural and planetary issues, as illuminated by dreams. The first column in this continuing series "Invitation to Interiority" naturally highlights the significance of interior dimensions and perspectives, which is also a recurring theme found within this issue. Based upon a dream of a series of nested boxes similar to the Russian dolls, Karen Jaenke presents an understanding of the sacred feminine defined as layered interiority. The nested boxes emphasize a progression towards smaller and subtler, hidden, interior spaces. Since patriarchal culture tends to focus on the exterior, visible dimension of reality, the orientation to interiority resides in the cultural shadow, widely overlooked and neglected. Yet from the interior perspective soulful depth and meaning are conferred onto life. Moreover, without the sensibilities of interiority, it becomes likely or even inevitable to damage the web of life.

Helena Daly's article, "Hypnopompic Encounter: Death's Shadow and Light between the Realms," brings to the forefront the importance of subtle consciousness, dreaming perception and the in-between hypnopompic realm. Through the application of a hermeneutic-phenomenological method of inquiry, this article presents and explores an extraordinary, transformative encounter with Light upon coming out of sleep. In significant ways, she differentiates the waking, hypnopompic state of consciousness from the hypnagogic state of consciousness that opens at the other end of the spectrum, prior to falling asleep. This third mode of reality, hypnopompia, highlights that higher states of awareness, embodied knowledge, healing, and the workings of soul and its relation to death and beyond, can be known and experienced.

Hypnopompic dreaming as a form of epistemological knowing is further illustrated and explored through a transformative experience of loving embrace upon awakening, in an article entitled "Heart Knowing and Dreams: Somatic Intersubjectivity." Daniel Deslauriers' scholarly personal narrative shows how inter-subjectivity is crucial in dream meaning-making, while simultaneously exploring the notion of trans-subjectivity (mirroring of image) and how this points to a preexistent and incipient knowing field—heart knowing. From within this field, latent potentialities and higher qualities and values that come through deep heart knowing (such as compassion, forgiveness and empathy), can be realized and actualized through a process of enactment. Deslauriers suggests that our embeddedness in the world is informed by how we embrace the world and are embraced back by it—an interrelated activity that shapes the world. While archetypal patterns and qualities of the world exist independently of us, as postulated by Jung's notion of the objective psyche, Deslauriers shows how these deep qualities accessed in dreaming and waking states, can come to be known only by enacting them, and by letting those qualities infuse our lives.

The transformative power of subtle

> *By consciously engaging states of contraction awakened by dreams, trauma's residue in the energy body is resolved, while shifting bodily constrictions towards spaciousness and joy.*

consciousness at work in the body is also explored in an article entitled "Dynamics of Expansion and Contraction in the Dreaming Body." Karen Jaenke, through a series of deep transpersonal dreams, with significant carryover into the waking state, describes and details how subtle dreaming processes when engaged within the hypnopompic state of consciousness, beneficially resolve the constrictions of trauma. Jaenke applies Eugene Gendlin's focusing method of attending to the *felt sense* as a guide to growth directions, showing how this method leads to expansive possibilities. By consciously engaging states of contraction awakened by dreams, trauma's residue in the energy body is resolved, while shifting bodily constrictions towards spaciousness and joy. Further, mindfully participating in the somatic dynamics of expansion and contraction conveys a keenly felt participation in the elemental dynamics of the universe. The hypnopompic state of being, therefore, can be recognized as a state through which dream energetics can be engaged and integrated, thus, accelerating the process of human growth at the energetic depths of our being.

Yet dreams intervene as a "daily nocturnal challenge to the paradigm of modernity/coloniality" and the presumed atomism of the self, instead revealing a self that is richly entangled with the world. Challenging the story of the Western masterful self, "Dreams re-introduce what has been excluded from awareness during the historical developments of the Western self. Moreover, for millennia, Indigenous traditions, have valued dreams as part of the shimmering and porousness of self. Dreams are an active presence in the Indigenous web of selves entangled in community and nature. The self revealed by dreams and embraced by indigenous traditions participates in a "complex osmotic pulsing between" interiority and exterior reality, yielding fresh perceptions, experiences and stories.

In conclusion, there is a need for more nuanced categorizations that map the rich complexity of actual dreaming experiences, in particular, the need for qualitative ethnographic accounts of higher dreaming types. The importance of dreams in the transpersonal context becomes crystal clear, and the pressing need for developing ever-deepening hermetic methods of inquiry. As this issue demonstrates, the theoretical implications of dreaming and the subtle consciousness awakened by dreams are far-reaching indeed, deserving careful attention. For dreaming fosters potential and actual long-term human development, embodied and actualized in waking life, while also addressing the limitations of the modern Western self.

References

A. E. (George William Russell). (1918). Candle of vision: Inner worlds of the Imagination. Dublin, Ireland: Macmillan Co. Press.

Bridge, U. (ed.) (1953). W.B Yeats and T. Sturge Moore: Their Correspondences. London: UK: Routledge & Kegan Paul.

Heidegger, M. (1926). Being and time. Oxford, UK: Routledge.

Irwin, L. (2015). Mystical knowledge and near death experience. In C. Moreman & T. Cattoi (Eds.), Death, dying, and mysticism (pp. 153–175). Basinstoke, UK: Palgrave.

James, W. (2005).Varieties of Religious Experience, Abington, USA: Routledge.

Kearney, R. (1998). Poetics of imaging: Modern and post-modern (Perspectives in continental philosophy). Bronx, NY: Fordham University Press.

O'Donahue, J. (1998). Anam cara: A book of Celtic wisdom. NY: HarperCollins Publishers.

Progroff, I. (1984). The cloud of unknowing. Alexandra, VA: Julian Press. (Original work published 1957).

Dreaming with the Collective:

Invitation to Interiority

Karen Jaenke, PhD

In a phenomenon identified by C.G. Jung as collective dreams, individuals dream about culturally-shared realities. "A dream with collective meaning is valid in the first place for the dreamer, but it expresses at the same time the fact that this momentary problem is also a problem of other people.... Every individual problem is also the problem of the age...." (Jung, Collected Works 10, par. 323). Such dreams have a collective meaning and people instinctively want to share them.

The commencement of this column, Dreaming with the Collective, foregrounds the special wisdom of dreams in illuminating our common cultural concerns. This column aims to tap into the wisdom of dreaming in addressing today's unprecedented societal and global issues. The shift in the Western orientation so urgently needed in our times, called the Great Turning by Joanna Macy and David Korten, refers to an epic shift from a 5000-year era of empires and earth domination to a new era of earth community; it can be fostered by attending to the undervalued perspectives of nighttime dream knowledge.

Rather than focusing on a particular societal or global issue, this piece addresses a sweeping one-sidedness, a root imbalance in collective life—the neglect of feminine ways of knowing and being. This deficit can appear in men and women alike, as it refers to an attitude, a predisposition, a perceptual and relational capacity, rather than to gendered bodies or roles.

In classic Western thought, the "feminine" carries connotations of receptivity and passivity, in contrast to the penetrating and active orientation of the masculine principle. Susan Griffin finds that running throughout Western philosophy and culture, women are associated with earth and nature, as life-giving sustenance (1978). This line of thinking originates with Plato's division of spirit and matter, where men and the masculine become associated with spirit and mind, and women and the feminine with matter, nature, earth and body (Griffin, 1978).[1]

In Eastern thought, yin-yang are two complementary forces in the universe emanating into all phenomena. Yin symbolizes earth, femaleness, darkness,

Photo: Karen Jaenke

passivity, and absorption, with yang connoting heaven, maleness, light, activity, and penetration ("Yinyang," n.d.). According to Taoism, both proceed from an original Unity, with their mutual interplay being responsible for the actual processes of the universe and all its elements. When operating in balance or harmony, the two principles are depicted as the light and dark halves of a circle, equal in size. Emphasizing the mutual interpenetration of yin and yang, the black half includes a white dot while the white half includes a black dot. The complementary relationship of yin and yang means that as one increases the other decreases, leading to situations of imbalance.

A dream of mine draws different contours of meaning around the feminine, and by implication, the masculine. In the dream, a reality outside familiar cultural structures—something foreign—breaks through, radically altering perceptions. Expressing this foreignness, the dream is set halfway around the world, in a distant land.

I am visiting a foreign country—India or Nepal—one of the cradles of ancient religion. I enter a small dimly-lit and tightly packed shop, filled with exotic sacred objects, too many for the eye to take in. The space is brimming with religious and symbolic figurines and items stacked on shelves lining the walls from floor to ceiling. Gold is present on many of the sacred objects, cohering the many discrete items, shapes and colors with a golden-themed hue.

A man is covering for the shop owner, who is a mysterious woman with a spiritual aura, away for the month. He is receiving and unpacking a newly-arrived shipment of

sacred objects. Among them is a small ornately carved sacred box, strikingly decorated with numinous stones. the box, which has caught my eye amid the myriad of things calling out, contains a series of boxes, housed one inside another, like Russian dolls. Each smaller box is more enchanting than the prior one, intricately carved and decorated with precious stones, arranged in receding layers of size and subtly. An overpowering fascination and spiritual yearning towards the specially-decorated boxes captivates me. I want to keep the boxes for a month until the shopkeeper returns, for they contain the fulfillment of my soul's deepest longing.

The foreign location halfway across the world suggests the rarified otherness of the dream environment. The female shop-keeper, a master collector and proprietor of scared objects, who casts a spiritual aura around her, but is herself hidden from view—away from the shop yet mysteriously present in the background—hints at the atmosphere of the sacred feminine.

The central captivating image is the numinous sacred box, a box of many boxes. Womb, chalice, and container are all ancient symbols of the feminine denoting the primal containing and gestating space of the womb, resurfacing here as the box (Neuman, 1972). These connotations of the feminine derive from the elemental form and function of the female body. Meanwhile, the numinous box-of-boxes, found inside her shop (which itself functions as a container for sacred objects), illuminates the essential structure of the sacred feminine—a hidden enclosure partaking of receding degrees of interior depth and subtlety.

Yet unlike the womb, in the dream there is not just one containing space, but a series of them. The dream presents a sequence of enclosures, one inside the other, in ever receding fashion. The boxes emphasize a progression towards smaller and subtler hidden, interior spaces. The nesting of boxes of diminishing size accentuate interiority. Not only is there interiority, there are greater degrees of interiority.

Rather than the classic connotations of passive/active, or receptive/penetrating, the dream redefines the essential feminine as containment and interiority, with the implication that the masculine is associated with exteriority—a distinction that in fact mirrors female and male genitalia. More fundamentally, exterior and interior denote two prime ways of orienting and organizing human consciousness, two alternative attitudes or approaches to life.

Let's look closer at these two aspects of the feminine, the containing function and interiority. First, the importance of containment and interiority are rendered invisible in patriarchal society. The chief evidence for the pervasive dismissal and disdain for the core feminine is the culmination of patriarchal culture in an environmental crisis endangering all life on Mother Earth. Disregard for the feminine equals disregard for the conditions under which life originates and thrives, in womb-like structures.

The womb is an enclosed space, a darkened environment, with a containing function; within this a protected space, creative things happen. Life requires a container, a protected space in which to grow and thrive. Psycho-therapists understand and adopt this principle as foundational to their craft and the psychological healing process. In order to heal the psyche of wounding, a safe and protected space is necessary, demarcated from everyday life, with its own special agreements and rules of operation. In patriarchal society this containing

---

Karen Jaenke, PhD Served as Chair of the Consciousness & Transformative Studies Masters degree program at National University (formerly John F. Kennedy University) from 2013 to 2022. In 2016, she launched and built the online modality for the Consciousness & Transformative Studies program, giving this cutting-edge program global reach. In 2021, she added to this leading-edge curriculum a Coach Training Program certified by the International Coaching Federation. Formerly, she served as Director of the Ecotherapy Certificate Program at JFKU (2011-14) and Dissertation Director at the Institute of Imaginal Studies in Petaluma, CA (2001-2008). An Executive Editor of ReVision: Journal of Consciousness and Transformation, she has edited journals and published articles on the topics of Imaginal Psychology, Shamanism and the Wounded West, Earth Dreaming, and Places of Hope, as well as numerous articles on dreams and consciousness. A repeat presenter at the International Association for the Study of Dreams, Society for the Study of Shamanism, and Science and Nonduality conferences, her creative vision synthesizes dreamwork, indigenous ways of knowing, subtle body awareness, living systems theory, and flow states.

function, whether physical or psychological, is often rendered invisible. Instead, patriarchal culture focuses on and celebrates the action or drama occurring the foreground, not the holding space in which action takes place. The container or space in which action occurs becomes backgrounded, largely imperceptible.

A second defining feature of the feminine, *interiority*, refers again to a space, one that is concave in shape, recessed, and hidden from everyday view, tucked away. The feminine attitude mimics the womb as a life-giving interior space with hidden depth. The interior aspect is accentuated by the profound alteration of consciousness that accompanies the dream. Upon waking, my awareness was descended and deposited, suctioned as it were, into the inner recesses of my body. In the dream's aftermath, my awareness emanates from the deep interiority of my body cavity, contrasting with a more typical surface or superficial awareness, hovering on the outer skin-layer of the self.

To grasp this notion of a receding interiority, consider several related images. Akin to the dream image of a series of nested boxes is the familiar Russian dolls, similarly stacked, one inside the other, suggesting diminishing degrees of size along with increasing of degrees of hiddenness and depth. A natural object partaking of a similar form is the onion with its many concentric layers, encircling a core. An everyday instance of retreating into a protected space or nested enclosure, occurs every night when we crawl under the layered covers of sheet, blanket, bedspread/comforter, with bedroom door closed, and outside doors locked tight. Similarly, when we lock our valuables inside a safe inside our closet inside our bedroom inside our house, we are participating in the same structure which conveys that what is most valuable dwells in a hidden place shrouded by many protective layers. An ancient symbol of layers leading to deeper interiority is the labyrinth, a pathway of concentric rings retreating to an innermost center.

Whichever image is adopted, an extended process is required to uncover all layers and reach the inmost center. The process of opening the Russian dolls cannot be done all at once, but requires a series of steps, repeated uncoverings.

Watching a young child unpack the Russian dolls for the first time, with utter fascination and bemusement at the repeating surprise of yet a smaller doll inside, sparks sheer delight! Through the eyes of a child, we reencounter the wonder of this mystery! The secrets of interiority, which partake of a range of depths, are not revealed all at once, but only through a process of successive engagement with diminishing scale yet increasing subtlety. When exploring interiority, the perceptual faculties that register slighter degrees of subtlety are awakened, just as a mediator discovers upon bringing sustained focus and concentration. The layers of mind open up hidden subtlety to a person persistent in attending to interiority, the building block of inner coherence.

Movement into interiority, with its mysterious realms and depths, and successive refinements of subtlety, is radically opposite the typical directional attention of American culture, with its pervasive "bigger is better" mindset, outward orientation, excessive stimulation of the senses, surface gaze, and superficial views. We see today's youth caving in under the pressures of surface appearances produced by social media.

> *The feminine attitude mimics the womb as a life-giving interior space with hidden depth.*

In mainstream culture, attention is constantly drawn and directed outward, skating across surfaces, constantly rebounding here, then there, with short attention span. Interior versus exterior gaze, as a fundamental orientation to life, then, applies not only to the attitude of an individual, but also the culture. Looking without versus within, as a basic predisposition, transmits into social orientations and societal organizations.[2] Historically, Asian cultures are more introverted, with Western cultures decidedly extroverted. "The inner life is the shadow of Western culture" (Kremer, 2023).

As a contemporary gauge of the predominance of the external attitude in Western culture, we need look no further than the Covid-19 pandemic. The virus brought a potential corrective along the interior-exterior axis of attention, with a socially-endorsed invitation to interiority, writ large across the entire globe. The necessity of social isolation to curb the spread of the virus delivered an unprecedented break in the status quo, with a rare opportunity to reorient lifestyle and attitude from exterior focus to interior.

> Physical lockdown and restrictions on our movement offered a unique opportunity for all of us to travel inwards and sit with ourselves. The external limitations also offered an opportunity to work on healing and renew our vision for a better future…. With the arrival of COVID-19, many people have been forced to take the inward journey…. [D]eprived of tools for distracting ourselves away from the soul's calling… [we are] forced us to listen to our deeper calling as we once did long ago (Soholm, 2020).

Instead, there was rampant ranting and kvetching in the streets against the limitations imposed by social distancing. The masses were utterly ill-prepared to enjoin a shift from outer to inner orientation. People struggled to make this life-saving adjustment of re-orienting their mindset and activities towards more solitary or interior pursuits, thus losing a special opportunity to grow a more balanced, complex, and resilient consciousness that can comfortably and happily move in the mysterious depths of the inner world, as well as the outer world.

The interior universe is equally vast as the exterior one, ever present for pioneering exploration and enrichment. An exclusively exterior sensibility predisposes us to extract all meaning, purpose and value from the external physical and social world, taxing the body of the planet. The unsustainable depletion of our physical environment is exacerbated because collectively we lack access to the richness of an interior universe of depth. We could relieve mother earth of the unrelenting pressure of our extractive excesses by delving into the interior universe, finding sustenance, meaning, depth, and fulfillment there.

When collective consciousness becomes exclusively driven towards outer goals and manipulations of the external world, without an equal anchoring in the depths of interiority, the interior-exterior balance of mental health and wellbeing suffers, along with the earth. A lack of embodied awareness, anchored in the deep recesses of the body cavity, leads to an absence of awareness of the invisible, intangible, subtle dimensions that infuse, animate and sustain life (Llamazares, 2018).

Without the sensibilities of interiority, it becomes probable, perhaps inevitable, to damage the web of life. Lacking a taproot into the substrate of interiority, people are prone to act in indiscriminate ways that unconsciously injure the delicate balance of life. All life forms partake of layers of depth and interiority. The modern, traumatized self with its surface gaze doesn't perceive these depths. Outer vision perceives external surfaces; inner vision perceives the interior depths. Only through accessing self-interiority can one imaginatively relate to the hidden interiority of another being. To the degree that we cultivate our own capacities of subtle sensing and perceiving, we are able to respect the subtle, intangible dimensions of other living beings. But when the outer world becomes the sole focus for deriving meaning and fulfillment, spread across an entire civilization, the delicate balance of living ecosystems becomes threatened.

How collective consciousness becomes disproportionately directed towards external pursuits merits further consideration. What causes attention to take on this excessive exterior drive, losing contact with the ground of interiority? The simple answer is trauma. In trauma, the mind-body system experiences a shattering jolt, and consciousness automatically ejects from the body. With dissociation, awareness no longer swims in the sensate body, but instead floats loosely around or above the body. Rather than circulating throughout the recesses of the body, awareness is re-positioned, in the zone of the head and outer surfaces of the body—or even detached from the body all together. Lacking tethering to the depths of interiority, the mind adopts a prevailing outward orientation towards life. Surface rather depth consciousness means a preoccupation with appearances and preponderance of superficial views. Along with dissociation and detachment comes numbness, loss of feeling, and inability to extend empathy to others.

Countering this up-and-out tendency, the boxes-within-boxes invite a staged descent into the interior underworld of the psyche, into the cavernous depths of the body. Instead of being projected outward, awareness turns and withdraws inward. The series of boxes depict the retreat of awareness into the hidden recesses of the body cavity and a progressive awakening of attention towards the small and subtle. The series of boxes symbolizes a series of interior spaces within the body, with its hidden chambers, recessed cavities, and cavernous depths.

If we embark on the interior journey, it will call for developing a capacity to attend to subtlety, being present to thought traces, faint feelings, and subtle sensations. The energy movements of the inner body register with about the same degree of lightness as a breeze grazing the skin. Transformative practices can aid in reorienting consciousness towards the interior pole. Embodiment practices, such as yoga, tai chi, and chi gong, bring conscious contact and communion with the subtle energies and deep ground of the body. Meditation funnels awareness in the inward direction. Attending to one's dreams offers an unparalleled path for connecting to the deep well of interiority.

Taking the redirecting hint of the dream, the ills that today afflict society, accumulating over the generations of male-dominated reign, find correction by a relative shift in orientation and attention from exterior to interior. According to the theory of complementarity, the excessive exterior gaze of patriarchal culture is rebalanced by cultivating interior sources of knowing, meaning and depth. The sacred boxes herald the possibilities of a different direction for humanity, one whose consciousness is not boomeranging on the surfaces of self and society, but quietly recedes into an interior exploration of the bedrock of being.

Endnotes

1 Yet under the distorted excesses of patriarchy, women also become receptive to male rage and victimization.
2 The interior-exterior distinction is formalized in Ken Wilber's Four Quadrant model, where the left side of the quadrant depicts interior, subjective perspectives, with the right side of the quadrant holding the objective, exterior perspective. In the horizontal direction, a dividing line between upper and lower quadrants differentiates individual from collective perspectives. Putting all four perspectives together:

upper left = individual subjective (interior or psyche)	upper right = individual objective (exterior or body)
lower left = collective subjective (culture)	lower right = collective objective (systems)

References

Britannica. (n.d). Yinyang. In Britannica.com. Retrieved October 20, 2022 from https://www.britannica.com/topic/yinyang).
Griffin, Susan. (1978). *Woman and nature: The roaring inside her.* New York: Harper & Row.
Kremer, Jurgen. (2023). "Dreams—Shimmering edges of self." *ReVision: Journal of Consciousness and Transformation*, Vol. 34-2, in Press.
Neuman, Erich. (1972). *The great mother: An analysis of the archetype.* Princeton, NJ: Princeton University Press.
Llamazares, Anna-Maria. (2018). "Wounded west: The healing potential of shamanism in the contemporary world." *ReVision: Journal of Consciousness and Transformation*, Vol. 32: 2-3.
Soholm, Helena. (2020). "When the ancestors call, how do we answer? Princess Bari, a heroine's journey." *ReVision: Journal of Consciousness and Transformation*, Vo
Wilber, Ken. (2001). *The eye of spirit: An integral vision for a world gone slightly mad.* Boston, MA: Shambhala.

Hypnopompic Encounter:

Death's Shadow and Light Between the Realms

Helena Daly, PhD

For most of my life, I have been pursued by dreams of mysterious and seductive powers and held an intense curiosity about psychic reality and deep dreaming experiences.

Photo above: Gary Newman
All others: Karen Jaenke

I have especially been acutely aware of those waking moments on coming out of sleep, while dwelling between dreaming and waking—a state of consciousness referred to as the hypnopompic state. This transient state of being that opens between sleeping and waking realms is a mysterious, deep, ephemeral and at times, highly charged state, full of moments made visible between the dark dead of the night and the dawning light of day—moments that leave as quickly as they came but not without leaving their mark.

During the early morning hours of January 20th, 2006, an indelible imprint was cast upon my body, mind and soul, following a profound healing experience upon awakening. I awoke to an encounter with Light—with ontological manifestations of living presence through which I experienced a deep affective life-death state of transformation. It felt as if a sacred contact had been signed, sealed and delivered with an innate force, with invisible presence seeking visibility and yearning to be born out of its own inner reality.

The far-reaching transformative effect of my encounter with Light, detailed here, helped lift me out of a depression, while going through a particularly difficult, painful time, and simultaneously changed the course of my life. Immediately following this transpersonal experience, I felt compelled to document all activity and associated phenomenology from that day to this, recording all nocturnal and waking activity in microscopic detail in a growing number of dreams journals—a discipline that developed into a committed spiritual practice. Seven months later, I left London, where I had been living at the time, and moved to San Francisco, armed with several dream journals tucked into my luggage, ready to study dreams in greater depth. And following a deep inner journey, gained my PhD in this precise area (California Institute of Integral Studies, 2016), exploring phenomenologically the hypnopompic state of consciousness and associated phenomena that manifests there.

These journals captured ordinary dreams (states through which inner processes are experienced and remembered) and different types of non-ordinary/transpersonal dreams—altered dream-waking states of awareness wherein subtle processes are reflectively observed with active absorption and self-conscious participation in and through them. My primary focus centered on transpersonal dream states—deep dreaming events that give rise to hypnopompic experiences and altered waking states of consciousness. This article is created around one such transpersonal experience, my encounter with light.

Given the focus of this article is the hypnopompic state, only aspects of the hypnagogic state are explored and discussed in relation to the dream-waking state, in order to help clearly identify and distinguish between these states of consciousness. In so doing, my aim is firstly, to provide an alternate way of approaching and understanding the hypnopompic state of consciousness; and secondly, that by considering the hypnopompic experience shared in this paper, along with ancient knowledge, depth psychological and transpersonal perspectives, the dream-waking state can be understood as a unique and important state of consciousness in its own right—a liminal, third mode of being through which healing, embodied knowledge, higher states of awareness, and the workings of soul and its relation to death and beyond can be known and experienced (Daly, 2016).

> *In this exploration, interpretation is rooted in an in-between realm that energetically unfolds, rising up from within an interior state that manifests through dreaming depth.*

Method

My thesis therefore, is rooted in a subjective premise, one that honors an inner epistemology grounded in experiential knowing (Heron & Reason, 1997). This naturally calls for hermeneutic-phenomenological methods of reflective exploration which holds a premise through which the art of interpretation is apt to yield unexpected insights, thus, helping challenge and transform preconceptions and older hermeneutical paradigms (Kearney, 1998).

The hermeneutic challenge of course, lies in the validation of interpretation and in distinguishing this from experience. So it is important to remember that interpretation is always highly contextual. This point needs to be emphasized! More general "objective" interpretations are garnered from the outside-in, without consideration from the inside-out—often a result of contempt prior to investigation. What is objective about that, I ask? Holding this in mind then, the reader can hopefully appreciate that it is the experience of particulars that alters perception, establishing therefore, an inner empirical basis of understanding and premise that does not claim general validity but offers new points of view for consideration.

In this exploration, interpretation is rooted in an in-between realm that energetically unfolds, rising up from within an interior state that manifests through dreaming depth. The art of interpretation in this context, therefore, follows a most subtle lead from the inside-out. This process unfolds through innate reflective structures and acute observation—deep reflection and critical thought based on experience. Revelatory embodied knowledge is imparted by entering fully the integral dialectics of hermeneutical experiences which are rooted in a bodily alertness that deeply listens, and attunes to the subtle threads of visceral, intuitive energetic resonance, and deep emotional undercurrents, all of which collectively allows meaning to unfold spontaneously without rational interference.

These forms of subtle consciousness are rooted in "body soul" (von Franz, 1998, p. 119), and it is through this subtle body that implicit meaning and significance unfolds. This way of knowing that comes through the visionary world of the dreamer is a type of empirical knowledge far removed from the measuring and testing of external perception (Irwin, 1994, p. 64). Subtle life transmitted through deep dreaming and waking states of being is a conscious intentional activity and movement from within, between and without that cuts across the usual dichotomy of subjective and objective. Hermeneutic methods of exploration and analysis work with existential dialectical processes as surely and as naturally as hand fits glove. And it is a powerful way of highlighting the function of interpretation: to make a type of fundamental existential disclosure, one that opens us to changes in our existence, in our dwelling (Levin, 2003, p. 27).

Offering a process-oriented perspective, neat, cushy, definite outcomes are not presented here. Instead, I offer revelatory insights that help raise questions, encourages speculative, reflective thought, and challenges the reader to recognize the difficulty and necessity of working with mystery. It challenges a different way of seeing and thinking that is situated in the middle, within a realm that manifests within mystery—within a multi-dimensional, multi-modal perceptive bridging state of consciousness between sleeping and waking realms.

The Dream-Waking State

The dream-waking state is a natural, ordinary yet extraordinary state of consciousness that plays a crucial role in helping to understand the phenomenon of dreaming as a potentially useful means of accessing knowledge and experiencing healing. *Ordinary* in the sense that everyone regularly passes through this state from sleeping to waking and *extraordinary* in terms of healing potentiality and actuality and as a gold mine for accessing information about subtle reality, death, and beyond. Yet today, this natural, ordinary yet extraordinary state of consciousness largely is forgotten, overlooked, misinterpreted and devalued.

The analogy of the ocean springs to mind as a way to reflect subtle realms of *beingness* from which dreams spring in their drive to manifest inner life, and as a way of describing the journey through sleeping, dreaming and waking states. The ocean is a common metaphor used within depth psychology as a way to represent the relationship between conscious and unconscious life, a small island rising out of an infinitely greater realm of unseen depths (James, 1990). I call this realm subtle reality—a realm accessible through sleeping-dreaming oceanic depth.

Ireland, as an island, forever strikes me as a geographical embodiment of this fluctuating relationship between conscious and unconscious life—where consciousness moves and flows along the continuum between water and land, night and day, sleeping and waking, darkness and light. Having been born and reared on the north-west coast of Ireland, land of the ancient goddess—that sits on the edge of one of the most westerly points of the European continent, I see her dimensional landscape, peripheral dwelling, and endless borderlands, as capturing the flow of visible and invisible life intermingling between the worlds. I offer this landscape, therefore, as a representation of the subtle state between sleeping and waking. A creative emerging unfolds between two primary modes—one rooted in the hidden realm of oceanic depth and darkness, and the other in the visible, physical, waking realm of light. Where these worlds overlap, there evolves a third elemental domain. A beach represents this beautifully—an intermediary ever-changing domain created between the elemental powers that be. This changing ground is neither water nor earth but a bit of both, with each domain needing the other in order to reveal itself from itself and to become something new.

Historical Context

In times past, in-between altered states and their existing landscapes, like the dream-waking states of consciousness, had long been recognized and explored through ritualistic practices. Eleusinian mysteries in ancient Greece and various shamanic and esoteric traditions and practices across cultures (Garcia-Romeu & Tart, 2013), as well as throughout the creative arts (Barrett, 2001), all recognized these states as holding enormous spiritual value and significance. These states were commonly referred to as the space-between-worlds—deeply receptive, liminal states of being, and places of heightened spiritual sensing wherein visions and big dreams carrying forth messages were received and experienced (Peat, 2005). Creative artists knew the semi-waking state as a potent, powerful, productive modality (Barrett, 2001), one through which infinite sources of inspiration, spiritual guidance and information in various forms was received (Keen, 1974).

Moments between sleeping and waking were identified as a "privileged state for experiencing divine revelation."

Mozart, for example, was believed to have heard and received entire pieces of music in sleep, before setting notes to paper, a phenomenon known as a form of eidetic hearing, a type of sight described as manifesting from within different types of non-ordinary states of consciousness that arise in sleep and between sleeping and waking (Swedenborg as cited in Lachman, 2009). This type of perceptual transmission, known to manifest from within different types of transpersonal states of consciousness that arise in sleep, is but one of many different types of sight (such as precognitive vision, clairvoyance, clairaudience) described throughout visionary traditions and practices (Swedenborg as cited in Lachman, 2009).

Iamblichus, for example, a third century Neoplatonic philosopher and practicing theurgist, described this state that opens between sleeping and waking as a waking condition through which divine dreams (denominated *theopemptoi* meaning "sent by the gods") were received and recognized. The divine origin of these special types of dreams were recognized as such by the presence of a clear voice that told precisely what was to be done, and that sometimes:

> A bright and tranquil light shines forth by which the sight of the eyes is detained, and which occasions them to become closed, though they were open before. The other senses, however, are in a vigilant state, and in certain respect, have a cosensation of the Light, unfolded by the gods (Taylor, 1984, pp. 116–118).

In further differentiating divine dreams from more ordinary dreams, Iamblichus describes this waking state in more detail, through which there occurs:

> a detention of the eyes, a similar oppression of the head, a condition between sleeping and waking, an instantaneous excitation, or perfect vigilance, are all of them divine indications, and are adapted to the reception of the Gods. They are also sent by the Gods, and a part of divine appearances antecedes according to things of this kind. (Taylor, 1984, pp. 116–118)

Centuries later, Swedenborg, an eighteenth century theologian and visionary, similarly described this waking condition, as a "spiritual state" (Lachman, 2009, p. 87). Moments between sleeping and waking were identified as a "privileged state for experiencing divine revelation" (Powell, 2018, p. 474). Swedenborg details transpersonal sight (visual and auditory) received in a state *midway* between sleep and wakefulness, and right at the time of wakefulness, when the dreamer is still waking up and sleep has not yet been fully shaken off. This state he refers to as "the sweetest of all, with heaven operating into the rational mind in utmost tranquility" (Swedenborg as cited in Lachman, 2009, p. 94).

Over time, in-between states and associated subtle life came to be known by many different names depending on one's perspective, thus, reflecting the elusive ground within which it stands—a fact of its deeper mystery. I suspect that this elusiveness has led to the dismissal, misinterpretation and misrepresentation of psychic reality and altered states of consciousness such as transpersonal dreaming and waking states of being. This on-going dismissal is still evident today, given the inability of science to deal scientifically with subtle consciousness, a fact that has greatly stifled the advance of psychology as a science (Progroff, 1957/1984, p. 10).

With the coming of the European Enlightenment period, also known as the age of reason, attempts were made to bring some defining status to altering states of consciousness. This shift ensured a movement away from a natural appreciation of the dream-waking state as a receptive state of being through which subtle perceptual life is transmitted, to more external, rational perspectives of consciousness.

Before coming to understand more fully then, the dream-waking state of being, and significant differences between the hypnopompic and the hypnagogic state, it is necessary to briefly compare and contrast mainstream western approaches (those rooted in the natural sciences) and non-western approaches to consciousness. Non-western approaches include eastern, ancient visionary traditions, depth psychological and indigenous perspectives on reality. These types of approaches to consciousness offer perceptual understanding through what I call *whole, circular approaches* to consciousness. What I mean by this is an approach that encompasses all forms of embodied perceptual activity transmitted day and night, above and beyond rational forms of knowing, thus, allowing for a deeper conceptual understanding of consciousness.

Approaching Sleeping, Dreaming, Waking States of Being and Subtle Life

In the West, the primary approach to consciousness is rooted in more rational concepts of consciousness, theoretical conceptualizations formed from the standpoint of the waking state—the standpoint of consciousness (Fromm, 1957). Western culture's monophasic orientation values only normal waking consciousness (Garcia-Romeu & Tart, 2013). The waking state is held as the dominant, normal state of being and the sole reference for how the world we live in is perceived and understood. These conceptualizations are built upon historical, learnt conditioning (Tart, 1975). They offer a limited perceptual insight and way of seeing that represents a consensus reality through a "specially tailored and selectively perceived segment of reality constructed from the spectrum of human potential" (Tart, 1975, p. 33). This narrow experience of the world can be understood then, as having little to do with the expansive range of human consciousness and more to do with mental constructs.

These conceptualizations of consciousness range widely depending upon different cultural values and perspectives, such as those cultures with a polyphasic orientation, in which diversifying altered states of consciousness are "embraced as a toolkit for the ultimate advancement of society" (Laughlin, MacManus, & d"Aquili, 1990; Whitehead, 2011). In western society, there is little consideration of the visible waking state as being but:

> one special type of consciousness, whilst all about it, parted by the filmiest of screens lie potential forms of consciousness, entirely different... against which our individuality builds but accidental fences, and into which our several minds plunge us in a mother sea or reservoir. (James, 1990)

These other potential and actual forms of consciousness are perceptual unfolding from the inside-out, transmitted from within transpersonal states that arise through sleeping and dreaming dimensions. However, with the coming of the natural sciences, these subtle forms of consciousness that open through dream and vision, were deemed meaningless and as having diminished association with divine messages and greater associations with mental illness and irrationality (Meier, 1986, p.106). Subtle phenomena received through sleep and dream were not and are still not understood as bringing to consciousness "their own

> *The enlightenment period, blinded and dazzled by its own solar power, cast a shadow over the more refined, subtle, lunar, emotive-intuitive, energetic ways of knowing.*

responses, experiences and significances," (Garrett, 1943, p. 48).

The enlightenment period, blinded and dazzled by its own solar power, cast a shadow over the more refined, subtle, lunar, emotive-intuitive, energetic ways of knowing. This heavy shadow served to diminish, extinguish and devalue visionary and dream states status as 'natural luminal states' (Jung, 1974). This shift marked the divide between visions and dreams' natural, spiritual grounding to more pathological perspectives that undermined the religious and spiritual function of dreams, thus, highlighting the development and dominance of more rational concepts of consciousness, and a progressive alienation from inner life.

Many contemporary thinkers, such

as those that hold a more materialist or rationalist view, offer objective, empirical insights into consciousness. This type of view reflects an outsider perspective—a perceptual life being lived more above ground, through the visible daylight realm of the human psyche (Jung, 1933),

> *Dreams were commonly held by early church thinkers, like St. Augustine, as primary avenues and valid conduits of spiritual revelation.*

one that seeks to explain, define and understand by means of intellectual and abstract reasoning. This more external, empirical perceptual understanding does not take into account perceptual transmission received from the inside-out, thus, bringing forth a different and limited kind of knowledge and meaning, one that does not reflect the greater complexity of human knowing, and that leads to existential alienation.

This is not to say that objective empirical insights on consciousness and altering states are not necessary and valuable. Dream research, for example, has benefited from neurological insight which has shown that "the usually dominant neocortex—the evolutionary recent and specifically human part of the brain, is inhibited during hypnagogic and hypnopompic states, and much older structures take over" (Mavromatis, 2010). These older evolutionary structures are attuned "to inner experience, and 'prelogical' forms of thought, using imagery, symbol and analogy" compared to cortical activity "associated with clear, logical thought and with the perception of a well-defined "external" world" (Mavromatis, 2010, p. 5).

This discovery, in my opinion, lends itself to C. G Jung's dream theory that claims the existence of innate biological anatomical structures—psychic formless structures known as archetypes (Neumann, 1974, pp. 81–82). The instinctual basis of these archetypes, when activated in deep dream states, bring forth collective memories, higher states of awareness, and energetic sources of deeply embodied knowledge, known and experienced upon awakening, as illustrated herein.

On the other hand, approaches to consciousness that incorporate non-rational aspects and other modes of knowing offer a perceptual understanding of the universe based on the standpoint of the unconscious, and consciousness has its roots there (Jung, 1933, p. 15) in dark sleeping depth. Approaches include depth psychological perspectives, ancient visionary, esoteric and yoga traditions and practices, as well as indigenous knowledge and wisdom.

Sleep in the ancient world was received as an oracle, "ready to be our infallible and silent counselor" (Synesius of Cyrene as cited in Fromm, 1957, p. 132). Sleeping-dreaming (non-ordinary) and waking (ordinary) states were held in ancient times as distinct states of being that offer different perspectives on reality (Fromm, 1957). The sleeping domain was understood as a mysterious ground of being (Peat, 2005)—a subtle yet deep realm of beingness associated with death and beyond, wherein the soul was believed to speak directly and guidance and divine healing received (Meier, 1989). Dreams were commonly held by early church thinkers, like St. Augustine, as primary avenues and valid conduits of spiritual revelation.

Greek mythological descriptions of sleep also speak to these associations between the sleeping domain, death and the life of the soul. Comparisons are made through brother gods *Hypnos* (sleep) and *Thanatos* (death) and death's sister in Homer's musing in the Iliad (as cited in Moody, 1975). This intricate association was also strongly held by Edgar Cayce, the great American sleeping prophet, who on the completion of his extensive lifelong work, declared the sleeping realm to be "a shadow of that intermission of life or that state called death". For Cayce, dreams were an avenue through which higher forms of awareness and perceptual knowledge about the death-state could be gained (as cited in Sechrist, 1968, p. 18).

These beliefs were also reflected through yogic and esoteric philosophies and practices. Yogic belief, for example, holds the sleep state, dream state and waking state as reflective of the three states of the soul. And esoteric literature describes these interweaving states through different bodies that operate—the *causal body* in deep sleep, the *subtle body* through dreams, and the *physical body* in the waking state. This subtle/dream body is also known as the *body light* (resurrected body) according to esoteric and gnostic belief and practice, *astral body* according to theosophists and yogis, (Powell, 1969), and *Soul* to Christian and Sufi mystics.

These interchangeable bodies/states of being (causal, subtle and physical) are believed to reflect the process of death and rebirth (Frawley, 1999)—altering bodies that represent interweaving worlds. From within the ancient Irish mind and Celtic cosmological perception, these worlds are

> *This subtle/dream body is also known as the* body light *(resurrected body) according to esoteric and gnostic belief and practice,* astral body *according to theosophists and yogis, and* Soul *to Christian and Sufi mystics.*

the *heaven world* (first world of archetypes, or white world), the *mid-world* (world of the water, characterized by constant fluctuation and shape-shifting), and *earth-world* (visible world and sensory perception) respectively (A.E., 1988, A.E. 1918, p. 78).

It is through the mid-world—a third mode of reality (Moriarty, 2005) wherein worlds overlap, that the Otherworld is accessed (Matthews, 1989; Whelan, 2010). This subtle realm opens *without* through dimensions inherent within the land (Matthews, 1989; Sheldrake, 1995; Stewart, 1992, p. 8), from *within* through sleeping-dreaming dimensions, and upon awakening *in-between* when realms overlap and changing bodies merge.

Paralleling these beliefs are depth psychological insights that view dreams and subtle states of being as opening within an intermediate realm of psychic actuality that teaches just what psychic nature really is. From within this subtle realm, the soul is believed to be freed from "its identity with the ego and the waking state" (Hillman, 1975a, p. 33) and insight granted into the soul's special relation with death (Hillman, 1979). This realm has been described as the *anima mundi* (the meeting place between spirit and body), an *interactive third* perceived symbolically which serves a transcendent function by which deeper meaning unfolds (Jung, 1964, 1974; von Franz, 1998).

Ancient visionary knowledge and depth psychological perspectives, therefore, can be seen to embrace hidden life and dimensions of experience. Perceptual unfolding transmitted through dreams' natural symbolic language and subtle energetic presence highlights the immense value of symbolic presence—much of which has been lost to the modern world. In the ancient world, the symbol was the means through which contact with the deepest self, with others and with god was made (Merton as cited in Osbon, 1991, p.283) and held as the key to a fundamental understanding of human nature and the world we live in, and as reflecting a more complete reality than can be encompassed in the rational concepts of consciousness (Neumann, 1974, p. 170). Indigenous cultures all over the world, for example, hold a deep reverence for sacred symbolic presence. Ancient dream perspectives are rooted within their symbolic character, understanding that "in exploring the ancestry of the symbolic vision we draw nigh to that clouded majesty we divine in the depths of our own being, and which is heard normally in intuition and conscience" (A. E., 1918, p. 69).

Furthermore, the importance of understanding symbolic language is highlighted when seeking to understand the development of personality (individuation). Individuation and transformative growth unfolds through a symbolic process—a process of psychic development (Jung, 1983, p. 21) depicted through symbolic expressive states received in deep dream states and associated altered waking states. This psychic transformation, I illustrate, through one such transpersonal dream-waking experience and unfolding hypnopompic encounter.

The dream-waking state of consciousness, rooted in the unfolding of subtle forms of consciousness that come through experiential components, can only be truly understood then, from within the ground of its own being, through letting the phenomena and unfolding inner constitution reveal itself from itself, without rational interference.

Coming to understand the deeper meaning and significance of the dream-waking state and associated phenomena does not come about through conventional scientific approaches and theories of reality but through circular approaches and explorative, reflective methods that take into account inner empirical ways of knowing, and that leave room for subtle life's mystery. When mystery is embraced, so too is the function of dreams' and visions' symbolic expression, which lies in transmitting meaning beyond rational levels of understanding—subtle transmissions that reflect a dynamism of existential and supra-personal significance, referable to a direct ontology (Perera & Whitmont, 1996).

The opposing dichotomy between approaches rooted in reason and rationalistic thinking, and more encompassing approaches that include non-rational aspects and bodily, multi-modal ways of knowing highlights, therefore, limited understandings of consciousness. It is vitally important then, when seeking to understand the dream-waking state of being, and subtle forms of consciousness, to approach this state in an open manner, one that recognizes the emergence of simultaneous realities through which a natural interconnectivity of unfolding perceptual life opens between darkness and light.

Deeper insight can be gained by drawing upon ancient visionary approaches to consciousness along with depth psychological approaches, which are grounded within a continuous whole circular movement between night and day, lunar and solar forms of consciousness—a circumambulation between the dark nocturnal realm of unconscious and subtle psychic activity and the visible daylight realm of the human psyche (Jung, 1933, p. 11).

Differentiating between the Hypnopompic and Hypnogogic States

While hypnopompic and hypnagogic states of consciousness are similar, given that both states open through subtle modes of consciousness along the continuum between sleeping and waking realms, thus, highlighting the interconnectivity between the conscious and unconscious mind, significant differences do exist. These transitional states are similar in that both states have been found through supporting literature from esoteric and occult practices, numerous experiential studies and spontaneous cases of parapsychological phenomena (PSI), to serve as a vehicle for extrasensory perception (Sherwood, 2002). Experiences of varying degrees that include visual and auditory features associated with precognition, telepathy, light phenomena, out-of-body experiences and apparitions (Mavromatis, 1987; Sherwood, 2002; Schacter, 1976; Gertz, 1983; Waters, 2016) are phenomena have that have been well-documented within hypnagogic literature—literature that tends to include hypnopompic experiences as part of the hypnagogic state.

This glaring tendency of researchers and writers across interconnecting fields of study, to not clearly differentiate between these states, naturally affects deeper understanding and interpretation. Yet there are important, distinguishing hypnopompic features that will be seen to highlight significant differences between these two states of being.

The hypnopompic state of consciousness is the state entered into on coming out of sleep while moving towards waking reality, while the hypnagogic state is entered into at the other end of the sleep cycle, when leaving waking reality and moving towards sleep. While the term 'hypnopompic' is sometimes correctly employed to describe the state that opens on coming out of sleep, it is more commonly used in contrast to the term 'hypnogogic.'

In the literature, hypnopompic experiences are consistently included as part of an overarching hypnagogic state. I suspect, this may in part be due to the

fact that the hypnagogic state is much better known and more commonly reported state of consciousness (Sherwood, 2002; Jaenke, 2004; Mavromatis, 2010), which naturally leads to this state being the more researched state. Experimentally and survey-based research on the hypnogogic state abounds with research findings frequently published in interdisciplinary fields of study, such as neuroscience, psychology, and consciousness studies. The hypnopompic state, on the other hand, is much less commonly reported with minimal research findings (Mavromatis, 2010; Sherwood, 2002; Jaenke, 2014).

In attempting to differentiate the dream-waking state from the hypnagogic state, the term *hypnopompia* was coined by Fredrick Meyers (1890), a classical psychologist and psychic researcher devoted to the study of consciousness and post-mortem inquiry. Its meaning derives from *hypnos* after the mythical Greek God of sleep and *pompe*, which means a "sending forth." The term *hypnagogia* was introduced years earlier in the nineteenth century by French psychologist L. F. Maury (as cited in Mavromatis, 2010) with the latter part *gogeus* meaning "leading" as in leading towards sleep. The technical reader will understand the hypnagogic state as rational waking cognition trying to make sense of non-linear images and sensations, and the hypnopompic state as dreaming cognition, emotionally incredulous, trying to make sense of waking reality.

A less technical and more open, fluid understanding of these altering states can be gained by calling to mind once again, the Irish landscape, one brimming with borderland places between water and land—interlinking spaces that bridge the unconscious and conscious mind. Entering the hypnagogic state prior to falling asleep is like starting a journey, slowly leaving land, getting ready to enter the ocean, about to venture into those depths and just beginning to feel the first wave or two through image and subtle sensation while moving towards sleep's depth. Moving out of sleep and deep dream states into hypnopompic consciousness is like returning from a long journey after having been at sea and travelling a great distance, awakening saturated with dream subtleties.

There is a softness and fluidity to coming out of sleep into the dream-waking state that is not so present and accessible at the other end of the continuum (exceptions to this sense of softness are when nightmares are experienced and waking becomes jarred). Realms of subtle life, collective sources of emotion, subtle energetic perceptual transmission and heightened states of altered awareness have been entered into while sleeping and in those liminal, hypnopompic moments are still accessible and experienced bodily. One way to think about the difference is to imagine the feeling when preparing with each shivering step and body tightening, a plunge into the ocean versus the invigorated feeling and a relaxed body after diving in and swimming like a fish.

This analogy highlights oceanic depth and rising emotional affect accessed and experienced through sleeping-dreaming dimensions, and upon awakening when dwelling between the states. Hypnagogic experiences, on the other hand, lack deeper experiential aspects and affect. It also serves to highlight how combining hypnogogic and hypnopompic states in the same category is like ignoring the difference between swimming on the ocean's surface (and becoming a bit acquainted with subtle activity), and swimming in the deep.

Yet, rarely, are these states differentiated. Frequently, experiences that clearly manifest upon coming out of sleep are referred to as "hypnagogic" visions (Lachman, 2009), which only leads to continual misrepresentation, misunderstanding and misinterpretation. Even the most comprehensive, extensive research to date on this subject matter (Mavromatis, 2010) does not differentiate between hypnagogic and hypnopompic states, and describes sleep dreams and day-dreams as being comparable in all aspects. This statement is not true and clearly reflects a lack of consideration of different types of non-ordinary sleep dreams. Transpersonal and archetypal dreams, for example, are deep dreaming events that give rise to hypnopompic experiences and encounters, the distinguishing, differentiating features of which we now turn to.

From within the dream-waking state, hypnopompic images arise from *internal sources* and come *fully formed* (McKellar, 1957) compared to hypnagogic images, which tend to form themselves in front of subjects, with eyes open or closed and are more *external* experiences. Hypnopompic images possess an *internal coherence* and *relational participation* not present within hypnagogic experiences which are much *more fragmented* and marked by a *general lack of participation* (Leroy, 1933).

Furthermore, hypnagogic states are also significantly characterized by a *lack of affective components* (Mavromatis, 2010, p. 206) and somatic elements (Waters, 2016)—central components of hypnopompic experiences that will be shown to serve a huge therapeutic and transformative role. The depth component and associated transformative affective power that comes through sleeping-dreaming spatial dimensions, highlights the important distinction between the hypnopompic experience and hypnagogic state.

...the dream-waking state is primarily a receptive state of being that arises through deep experiential knowing and associated transformative affective components that serve a huge therapeutic role.

In my view, informed through my own dream practice observations and experience, as well as my understanding of the literature, I believe a hypnagogic state manifests in a similar way to day-dreams with dream-like phenomena, wherein surface mental imagery and levels of awareness are played with. To my mind, this state of being is comparable to more ordinary types of dreams in which inner processes are observed without becoming absorbed in them, thus, reflecting more of a cognitive sensing and experiencing. This type of state then, could be described as more reflective of an "intellectual state" (A. E., 1918).

Hypnagogic explorers, such as the twentieth century Danish philosopher, Mosikivin as cited in Lachman, 2009), and the Russian mystic philosopher and spiritual teacher, P. D. Ouspensky (1974), knew the hypnagogic state as one through which the preservation of awareness could be practiced, and double consciousness—waking and dreaming experienced. From within this practice, some degrees of control could be exerted over dream-like phenomena—discoveries that led to the development of techniques for deeper exploration in lucid dream states.

While double consciousness also operates from within the hypnopompic state, the manifestation of this state does not come about as a result of controlling and manipulating dream imagery, a crucial and significant difference. This dream-waking state manifests through letting the emerging dream phenomena be, without rational interference, thus allowing powerful experiences to naturally emerge. Transpersonal dreaming events are experienced through a deeper absorption and participation that hold great transformative potentiality and actuality. This type of dreaming experience, rooted in experiential states of being that give rise to hypnopompic experiences upon awakening, is therefore very different from hypnagogic experiences that do *not* arise out of inner depth and dreaming spatial dimensionality.

Understanding this depth component and subtle activity transmission, from within sleeping and dreaming domains, is key to understanding the significant and meaningful differences between hypnopompic and hypnagogic states. Dream-waking encounters and hypnopompic consciousness are experienced through unifying symbols within "conflicting *autosymbolic tension*" (Silberer, 1965). A meaningful awareness of the significance of symbolic presence in the hypnopompic state is keenly felt, the awareness and implicit understanding of which is largely absent in the hypnagogic state. From within this waking experience, the tension and conflict that naturally exists between a stable consciousness and a charged unconscious is experienced. These simultaneous realities (the dark night world and day world of light) oppose one another, thus, reflecting the tense inner-outer merging through which dream-waking states emerge.

This enormous tension—high creative energy when endured, brings about an energetic transmutation (Neumann, 1974, p. 19) through which a state of suffering is called forth, one that gives birth to the *third state*. While hypnagogic states also manifest through tension, it is a very different kind of tension, one produced between "drowsiness and an effort to think" (Silberer, 1965) wherein the conscious ego remains alert and interacts with the vision. Creative tension experienced within hypnopompic states manifests within conditions of much greater drowsiness and an effort *not* to think, through the suspension of egoic activity, withdrawal of mental activity and preservation of psychic energy and being with whatever arises, without control or manipulation.

This third in-between state that manifests between sleeping and dreaming realms, is a state of being then, that does not compare to the hypnagogic state in significant ways. While both states are receptive modes for subtle forms of consciousness and varying degrees of extra-sensory perceptual transmissions, the dream-waking state is primarily a receptive state of being that arises through deep experiential knowing and associated transformative affective components that serve a huge therapeutic role. The combined activity of these distinguishing features that open in sleep and lead to hypnopompic experiences upon awakening, emphasize therefore, important intrinsic characteristics that highlight transpersonal dream states experienced in sleeping-dreaming dimensions as distinctly different from dream-like phenomena that opens in the hypnagogic state.

The following hypnopompic experience demonstrates this deep receptivity and the inner, intrinsic working of subtle perceptual transmissions received through multi-modal senses from within this third state of being. These include creative, visual, symbolic, visceral, proprioceptive and kinesthetic channels, and energetic, emotive, intuitive and rational modes of knowing.

Tunnel of Light: Love

I open my eyes on coming out of sleep and find myself encased in the most exquisite, soft, golden light that transmits tremendous, inexplicable tenderness. As I lay there, soaking up this healing light, I feel deep bliss move through every cell in my body and feel as light as a feather. I become aware that I am receiving this light in a tunnel made of light and as I am being moved into it, start to experience a tremendous love of indescribable magnitude.

While being perfectly aware of my sleepy body on my bed, I enter even more deeply this tunnel of light between sleeping and waking realms. A witnessing self observes my dreaming/subtle body move through a circular opening into this perfectly round tunnel. I move

> "I become aware that I am receiving this light in a tunnel made of light and as I am being moved into it, start to experience a tremendous love of indescribable magnitude."

slowly along, flying low down close to the tunnel ground, never touching it but hovering just above it. I observe with extreme care this place I am in, an ethereal circular tunnel made of the most subtle, golden light imaginable. I can see straight ahead of me for at least a mile or so and see the brightest, whitest light at the very end of this tunnel, its pure, white, dazzling brilliance contrasting to the yellow, luminous tender gold light that surrounds me. I do not look ahead for too long, turning my head instead to the tunnel walls where some etchings and engravings catch my eye.

I fly the tiny distance to the tunnel wall which is within arms' reach of the center, and observe my dreaming body move from horizontal low flying to vertical hovering. I touch this transparent wall of light and inspect it, surprised to find some structural solidity there within darkened, concentrated light. I trace with my fingers many engraved symbols and feel wonder and excitement. While hovering in front of the wall, I note that my vertical stance is restricted because it is not possible to extend to my full height (5' 8"). I observe my legs automatically coming up and taking the position of a ninety degree angle as if seated upright in a chair ready to inspect and examine the wall. I suspect at this point that the tunnel could not be more than 4-5 feet in height and that the only way to travel this tunnel would be to fly through it. To the right of these symbols, I see what looks like another language hidden in the darker recesses of the tunnel wall light. I examine it in utter amazement as it starts to dawn on me that this language is even older than its neighboring symbolic language. The symbols were a mixture of etched drawings and shapes while this older language looked more numerical, with lines and dots. One section consisted of short and long rows of singular chalk-like line markings, some of which had dots over them. It felt to me that this was perhaps a sentence, with each stack of lines and dots making up a word. I hover there in total awe before feeling and observing my subtle body move back into a horizontal position. I experience waves of love so deep and beauty so great wash over me. I bask in this radiance and feel a deep yearning to sleep here, to lay in this fiercely loving, gentle presence forever. I am reluctant to close my eyes, afraid that this will leave me and I will return to ordinary light and full waking consciousness.

As my eyes close the light fades and I start to become more fully aware of my waking-self lying perfectly still in bed. I feel the softness of my bed and looking up to my right, glimpse dark light peeking through my window, night-light moving towards twilight and I start to cry in painful recognition of having returned to physical reality, to ordinary light.

I experience intense waves of sadness and longing, peace and wonder, and I cannot stop crying. It is as if an inner dam has burst and water washes through me like a river of healing water that is cleansing the very depths of my soul.

Upon awakening, while becoming aware of this light that folded in around me, I became aware of a tremendous lightness of being. Through this, movement opened that enabled simultaneous, heightened, lucid awareness and acute observation of physical and subtle realms, and deepening exploration of the light's form and texture. As movement within the realm of light progressively deepened, a deepening in affect was also experienced. Powerful healing features were intimately experienced throughout my whole being; shimmering goldenness, immense tenderness, lightness of being, bliss, pure unadulterated love of great magnitude, and exquisite, immeasurable beauty that held no bounds, above and beyond anything I have ever experienced at the human level.

While flying within this golden light, I observed another strand of Light at the very end of this tunnel; pure, snow white, blinding light compared to this softer, transparent golden light that enveloped me. While taking in these contrasting forms of Light, I also observed dense elemental structures hidden within the darker recesses of the golden tunnel wall. Changes in kinesthetic movement (inner movement of consciousness) of the dreaming subtle body, from horizontal to vertical hovering, allowed for closer inspection to be carried out. A ninety degree right angle was formed, an alignment that represents partial intersection between horizontal and vertical domains within this sacred realm of light. Through this intersection the subtle body is upright for the first time and maintains a hovering position through which the first and only point of physical-subtle contact with this elemental light is made, a deeper contact that came through the hands.

The importance of this discovery implicitly registers through feelings of surprise, excitement, awe and wonder, emotions often described as religious emotions (Otto, 1928/1958), the resonating effect of which alerts me to their ancient status. Here, from within another subtle realm of existence, I am shown traces of human activity. This particular activity, precisely laid out lines and dots in short and long stacks, the visual of which is as clear in my mind now as it was then, I came to discover, is an ancient language—a numerical system identified with the Maya Indians of Guatemala and other Mesoamericans (Carasso, 2012), and quite possibly other ancient sources as well. This astonishing discovery came to me, through my dissertation reader, Lee Irwin—a scholar of Native American Visionary Dreaming Traditions.

This significant discovery is deeply important given that evidence of this primal language is connected to evolutionary stages of consciousness, to times when different symbolic language systems were the pertinent way of communicating. It is possible, therefore, that this discovery within dreaming subtle reality may be showing some origin points in the history of human symbol making. As the full effect of these revelations sink in, I experienced intensely, again, the core phenomenological features of this primal light; shimmering goldenness, tremendous love, powerful gentleness, peace, radiance, heightened lucidity, bliss, profound beauty and incredible lightness of being, before observing my dream body move back into the horizontal position in preparation for the transition back to physical reality.

> *This primal light lit up my interior chambers as surely as a single candle lights up a dark room, the energetic power of which reconfigured my whole being, bringing to an end that time of darkness.*

The transformative healing power experienced through this elemental, numinous encounter with light, within such a refined, sacred, subtle dimension of reality, served to bring me out of inner darkness and density and into lightness and possibility. This primal light lit up my interior chambers as surely as a single candle lights up a dark room, the energetic power of which reconfigured my whole being, bringing to an end that time of darkness.

Application of Theory and Research Discoveries

In light of Jungian theory, the working of a natural law of psychic happening, of *compensation* (Jung, 1974) between conscious and unconscious domains, is evident here. The psyche's automatic self-regulation balanced a depressed, dark conscious attitude with the overflowing, energizing encounter with light. This undiluted encounter with light, also highlights subtle activity that opens above and beyond this compensatory function, through the manifestation of unintentional aspects that are known to open within higher states of being that point to "an intelligence and purposiveness which are superior to actual conscious insight" (Shafton, 1995, p. 109). These aspects can be perceived through diffuse intuitive knowledge that reflects our being (von Franz, 1998), thus drawing attention to the deeper unreflectiveness of a reflective consciousness (Heidegger, 1926; Merleau-Ponty, 1962/2006).

According to Jungian theory, the insightful depth of this experience between the realms suggests the intimate working of *archetypes*, collective psychic structures or energetic forms/patterns believed to contain the collective memory and wisdom of humankind (Neumann, 1974). Archetypal forms are thought to represent intersection points between personal time and timeless transpersonal being (Grosso, 1994) or chronological and dreamtime—*distentio animi*—an extendedness of the soul (St. Augustine as cited in Arden, 1994). This particular hypnopompic encounter unfolds through these overlapping, deep dimensional openings, manifesting as it does between sleeping, dreaming and waking realms, between a "vertical timeless axis crossing the horizontal flow of time" (Blake as cited in Northrop, 1966, p. 24). This experience, therefore, can be understood as one that reflects higher active, energetic, dimensional principles of dream space at work within a liminal, transitional state of being through which cosmic healing interconnections are made.

Archetypal function is to assist the growth and evolution of humans, be that during a major crisis of individuation (Grosso, 1996) or when moving through what is perhaps the greatest transition of all, dying and death (Perera, 1981). The instinctual basis of these deeply rooted structures when activated in deep dreams states (as mentioned earlier in line with recent neurological dream research), bring forth collective memories, higher states of awareness, and energetic sources of deeply embodied knowledge.

This transformational experiential encounter strongly parallels descriptive accounts of near-death experiences (NDEs) and out-of-body experiences (OBE's) widely recorded within death and dying literature. An OBE, also referred to as "extra corporeal perception" (ECP) represents a primary locus of awareness in the in-between state through which a dynamic process in which a non-physical self, manifests (Irwin, 2015).

Although the experience relayed here did not arise through actual physical death followed by a return to life, nor does it reflect any suicidal thoughts or ideation, it does reflect a profoundly life changing experience within a realm of light and ineffable, penetrating beauty that emerged through the depths of dark psychological and emotional pain that was inwardly killing me. This dark inner landscape is reflected in Greyson's (2000) description of NDE's as "profound psychological events with transcendental and mystical elements, typically occurring to individuals close to death or in situations of intense physical or emotional danger" (pp. 315-316). My turbulent inner life could be described in terms of emotional danger, which transformed through "inner light," a profound realization described as a mystical form of enlightenment similar to higher forms of NDE's (Bhattacharya, 2014).

Ray Moody's (1975) extensive research on NDE's and recent paranormal, transpersonal and mystical research, detail narrative accounts that reveal similar encounters with light. Overarching features, such as seeing a light during NDE's as well as perceptions of merging with this light or the source of being-ness (Facco, 2012); of entering the light, leaving the body, and intensified feelings of deep peace typically characterize NDEs (Blackmore, 2004, p. 360).

The experience of extraordinary vivid physical sensations, ESP and precognitive visions are experiential aspects in deeper NDE experiences that have been described as a "cosmic encounter with light, God, or other manifestations of great ontological import" (Irwin, 2015, p. 3). "Light" is the primary symbol of all great religious traditions thought to reflect the manifestation of God, and has been spoken of by theologians and mystics as an energy that is "known in the mind, felt in the heart, sensed in the body, and that comes from, and is, Spirit" (Metzner, 1998, pp. 165–169).

The progressive movement in this in-between state of being has been described within a particular type of hypnopompic state that resulted in the experience of "not knowing whether one was in the body or out it" (Swedenborg as cited in Lachman, 2009, p. 94), thus, reflecting paranormal and transcendental aspects comparable to an out-of-body experience (Irwin, 2015). There exists a wealth of widely published paranormal research, grounded in personal narratives which detail non-ordinary states of consciousness, such as near-death experiences and out-of-body experiences, accepted and recognized as empirical sources of data (Tart, 1997; Greyson, 2006; Irwin, 2015). Empirical findings in parapsychological research consistently show that people who attend to internal states such as meditative and deep dream states "open up sensitivities that can detect and receive nonlocal universal intelligence such as extra sensory perception" (Tart, 1997, p. 108).

In-between experiences within voids and tunnels are also well documented (Greyson, 2006; Irwin, 2015; Ring, 2006; Tart, 1997). While the tunnel experience is mostly associated with and reported by near-death experiencers, this type of experience has also been reported to happen during an OBE not associated with physical near-death experiences, spontaneously, through hypnosis and trance state, or under the influence of psychedelics (Sellars, 2018; Blackmore, 2004). This begs consideration around whether tunnel experiences occur not only during the process of dying, but also as an organic part of other phenomena such as time travel or quantum tunneling (Sellars, 2018).

Greyson's fourfold typology of NDE's describes lucid movement through tunnels or velvet darkness, heightened awareness of local physical surroundings along with movement away from them, and encounters with a non-ordinary realm inhabited by postmortem others (friends, family, and "beings of light"). This typology details cognitive, affective, paranormal, and transcendental features of these experiences, as well as enhanced abilities and an intensification of feelings (Beauregard, 2011; Garcia-Romeu, 2010; Johnson & Griffiths, 2011, Levin & Steele, 2005). Transcendental dimensions are held as spatial domains wherein the soul subjectively senses and picks up important information received through visual and auditory transmission (Cayce

> *"Light" is the primary symbol of all great religious traditions thought to reflect the manifestation of God, and has been spoken of by theologians and mystics as an energy that is "known in the mind, felt in the heart, sensed in the body, and that comes from, and is, Spirit."*

as cited in Sechrist, 1968)—veridical information, obtained through "empirically evident paranormal perceptions" (Irwin, 2015, p. 16).

Increasing lucid awareness, an exceptionally strong feature of my hypnopompic encounter, ensured a deepening of this experience into transpersonal and mystical domains (Stumbry, 2018). It is through this exceptional lucid quality, that some insight into the nature of consciousness is granted, particularly through the natural emergence of self-reflection and meta-awareness capacities (Stumbrys, 2018). And this is how I understand lucidity—as a quality of consciousness which contains innate self-reflective properties of reflexivity, foundational to consciousness (Irwin, 2015). While this encounter was profoundly lucid, the intrinsic, intricate working of this lucid presence was received differently to how lucid dreaming is commonly received and understood.

Lucid dreaming is commonly referred to as "being aware that you are dreaming when you dream" and using this awareness to change/shape the direction of a dream, or its potential outcome. While being very much aware of what was unfolding throughout this deep encounter, the increasing, lucid awareness served to sustain this heightened awareness and my being a lucid, participant observer of what was naturally unfolding, as opposed to trying to direct or manipulate any type of outcome. By allowing this subtle realm to unfold from within its own reality, without any kind of imposed control, through focused attention and acutely tending to what arises, any deeper emergence of significant ontological import is not prevented from coming through (Irwin, 2014). Heightened and deepening lucidity, therefore, can be understood as opening self-healing properties (Sellars, 2018). This potent awareness acts as a form of mediating awareness that links sleeping, dreaming and waking states of being, and as a medium for the cultivation of a more complex awareness and heightened sense of participatory engagement with profound possibilities (Irwin, 2014).

Intensification of feelings and deepening in affect came through a deepening lucidity, as I travelled deeper into the tunnel of light. Perera's (1981) describes this profound affect commonly experienced within transpersonal encounters as an unfolding process of recollection

and remembrance—one that reflects a consciousness born of suffering and loss. The profound sadness I experienced on returning, having crossed over into this sacred, healing realm of light, love and beauty, reflects perhaps a sense of separateness for the loss of this unifying state of bliss (Perera, 1981, p. 71). My sorrow was accentuated by the fact that while not truly wanting to die, I was acutely aware that I was returning to a life I had always struggled to live and fully participate in.

Accounts of the transformative effects described here, along with core phenomenal features, and paranormal dimensions (Ring & Valerion, 1998) are consistently reported cross-culturally. The aftereffects of this type of NDE encounter, as with OBEs have been widely reported as highly transformative, affecting an increased sense of spirituality, concern for others and decreased fear of death (Greyson, 2000), and a positive, dramatic shift in personality and worldview (Irwin, 2015)—all of which I can personally testify to, following my hypnopompic encounter with Light. The occurrence of veridical psi components and huge long-term transformative effect experienced within this particular type of in-between state, and its' strong associations to NDE experiences, counter criticisms that perceive this type of experience as a delusory one.

Furthermore, this type of in-between, out-of-body tunnel experience, is frequently presented within scientific theories and particular perspectives such as a psychophysiological one, as representing a flashback to the birth canal process, thus drawing an analogy between the birth process and death process. However, the essential structures of birth and death experiences are quite different and the reverse of one another. The birthing passage "moves from amniotic bliss to expulsion into traumatic light" (Grosso, 1996), a process of expulsion quite contrary to universal and cross-cultural descriptions of flying and a lightness of being within this tunnel. The dying process, on the other hand, often begins with elements of pain, fear and shock, followed by experiences of a light described as warm, loving and gentle (Grosso, 1996). In recent near-death studies, ninety percent of individuals reported going into the light.

These discoveries and components of phenomena that speak to its universality, paranormal dimensions, and deep transformative effects, are empirical facts that continue to support an archetype of death

(Grosso, 1996; von Franz, 1986), thought to represent passages and subtle realms of existence between dying and death (Moody, 1975). Psychical research, points to real possibilities of the continuity of consciousness after death, opening great avenues that extend beyond physicalist accounts of the universe (Irwin, 2015). This particular, liminal, transitional dream-waking state of being, therefore, can be understood as one that manifested within an energetic open realm of potentiality with associations to other transitional states between life and death and death and beyond (Perera, 1981, p. 72).

This revelatory hypnopompic encounter, therefore, carries profound symbolic, psychic, epistemological, ontological, methodological, psychosomatic, and psychosocial implications that impact inter-disciplinary and intra-disciplinary schools of thought and practice.

Implications

Symbolic

Deep exploration and understanding of symbolic expression that opens through dreaming and waking states, highlights significant phenomenological outcomes that result in a deepening, developing familiarity with altered, diversifying states of consciousness. Implicit to this developmental understanding is an appreciation for the psychic value of altered states of consciousness and their important role in helping understand how healing happens.

Deep dream states and altered waking states are symbolically expressive states through which "a process of psychic development" (Jung, 1983, p. 21) unfolds. This symbolic process, shown to be at work in the development of personality (individuation), highlights the importance of understanding symbolic language, given individuation and transformative growth has always been and remains to be, depicted in symbolic form and expression (von Franz, 1998). When this process is taken consciously, consciousness confronts the unconscious and a balance between the opposites is found.

Consciously engaging with night-life, with nocturnal symbolic life, invites a deepening relationship with the other side of reality, through which transformative states of being emerge. Understanding the importance of hidden life

lies in the fact that it is not possible to effectively bring about forms of healing and treatment from the daylight side of consciousness (Jung, 1933, p. 16); rather this must come through "dark cythonic depth" (Meier, 1989, p. 127), wherein lie dreams' symbolic life and autonomous healing powers.

Epistemological

This inquiry highlights the importance of dream consciousness and points to the phenomenon of dreaming and waking states of consciousness as actual and potential means of accessing higher states of awareness, embodied ways of knowing, healing and knowledge about the workings of the soul and its relation to death and beyond. Learning how to work with and assimilate subtle consciousness that comes through dream-waking states (in varying measure and degree of intensity) leads to fundamental insight into psychic life, thus contributing significantly towards the development of the faculties of inner life and innate epistemological sources of knowledge. Hypnopompic ways of knowing come through a receptive waking condition of relaxed alertness, focused attention, acute observation within and through participatory modes of being, deep listening, and resonating, emotional, intuitive energetics. All aspects of developmental unfolding, are then reflected upon in terms of a model of human potential.

Ontological

Inner dream space spilling forth upon awakening opens up the possibility of an exploration of powerful encounters with being. It proposes a meta-physics of being within the heart of interiority. This recovery and recollection unfolds through hermeneutically attending to dream-waking gaps—to the interconnecting spaces that join visible and invisible life. Here, in the in-between space, symbolic, physical and subtle consciousness are interwoven, all of which are considered different manifestations of the same metaphysical principles (Evola, 1971). From within the in-between state, consciousness itself becomes transparent and transpersonal archetypal structure is shown as a living process that unfolds from within its own realm.

This unfolding of deep, divine relatedness and interconnectivity between invisible and visible domains has important implications for understanding our psychophysical nature and the world about us. Knowledge of this liminal third state, which separates what we see presently and what lies hidden through the earth, is a knowledge shared by all ancient cosmologies and the view of reality held by mystics of all traditions (Smith, 1992). It is possible then, that the dream-waking state and associated hypnopompic phenomena is a state of being that opens, however briefly, into *Unus Mundus* terrain—a domain that seeks to reveal itself while concealing itself within deepening dialectics of the *mysterious coincidentia oppositorum* (Wedemeyer, 2010). This subtle realm is believed to be instrumental in the divine teleology of human existence that provides the intermediate ground for the merging of a transcendent God and earthly being (Jung, 1964).

> *Understanding the importance of hidden life lies in the fact that it is not possible to effectively bring about forms of healing and treatment from the daylight side of consciousness...*

Subtle life and subtle forms of consciousness, therefore, imply a survival of consciousness—one that is ontologically no less real than physical reality on the one hand, and spiritual or intellectual reality on the other (Corbin, 1972). This transpersonal experience reflects a multi-dimensional unitary consciousness, accessible through the dream body that bridges the mind-body-spirit continuum, thus addressing dualism in western thought, and the spirit-matter dichotomy. Deep consideration of this possibility highlights the need for further exploration and mapping of transpersonal dreaming encounters, subtle states, altered bodily states of awareness that "deconstruct subject-object modes in favor of profound participatory knowing and being" (Jaenke, 2004b, p. 13). To do this, rather than come to know more and more about dreams, we want to get "deeper into dreams by working out ever more penetrating and subtle forms of inquiry"—namely, hermetic methods of inquiry (Hillman, 1979, p. 201).

Methodology

Approaching dreams as revelatory phenomena and the hypnopompic realm as a revelatory state provides a fresh new way of seeing and perceiving. It naturally applies itself to a hermetic field—one that is self-contained and self-generating that opens through powerful symbolical expression upon awakening. Embracing the hypnopompic realm as an energetically emerging third mode of being, or post-dual third that sits in the middle—within continual, dynamic, opposing tense interaction between psyche and soma, fluid invisibility and condensed visibility, allows for the synthesis and reconciliation of apparently separate elemental realms.

This working dialogical approach is in line with current concepts of consciousness that take into account reflexivity inherent in full experience that cannot be split or reduced. It works with extreme whole body states, and demonstrates a coming into being not through abstract reasoning alone but through a deeply embodied practice. This way of working offers a natural, more complex way to explore generative states of inner, between and outer reality that holds within its interiority transpersonal depth and archetypal structures and visions. It encompasses multiple forms of subtle consciousness, helping balance more rational and materialistic external scientific perspectives, that has shaped and continues to shape how we make sense of reality.

This approach naturally applies methodological techniques that describe critical ways of experiencing reflectively from within embodied states of being, thus serving as a post-dual way of knowing that goes beyond the mind-body split. Deep, reflective experiencing of transpersonal states and rich documented descriptions of subtle phenomenal unfolding help, therefore, in the development of a science of subjectivity—while highlighting how grounded revelatory insight and knowledge shows the complexity of human perceptual unfolding, in potentially and actuality. In laying out the experiential groundwork, the interrelationship between mental and physical processes is illustrated, thus highlighting how deep psychological exploration and critical reflective methods of analysis help bring forth greater understanding of subtle life and naturally occurring altered dreaming and waking states.

A dialogical way of seeing and understanding also serves to help in the development of a theory of attention and reflection. A theory of attention is important given that deep concentrated attention (awareness) and swirling psychic energy are at the very heart of this reflexivity, and that even small shifts in attention open out revelations of "the extended range of our true self" and nonlocal consciousness that allows for direct knowing (Tart, 1997, p. 141). Deliberately attending to, is powerful activity consistently shown to empower the visionary ability (Cressy, 1996). This active technique offers a way to access, develop, and activate paranormal perception and ability, highlighting how innate potential can be developed and actualized. The cultivation of focused thought and attention is central to diversifying mystical techniques and contemplative practices. Therefore, with a view to future methodological developments, training in attention can be seen to be crucial to unlocking, accessing, exploring, developing, and enhancing human perceptual abilities (Irwin, 2015, p. 10).

Psychosomatic

Committed dream work is a transformative psychosomatic healing practice, through which the somatic unconscious, the part of the unconscious which becomes more and more identical with the functioning of the body, becomes accessible through the dream body upon awakening. It is through the body that inner life is accessed, and non-ordinary and higher cosmic perceptions explored and known (Irwin, 2015, p. 14). Thus, bringing forth the fruits of embodied, subtle life is "crucial for the actualization of deep consciousness potential" (Irwin, 2015, p. 18), and central to the unfolding and development of healing power at work. The body, therefore, serves as the central channel through which healing processes emerge, and through which the deeper integration takes root.

Interdisciplinary Connections and Considerations

Archetypal Psychology

This article, in bringing forth a detailed description of dream-waking phenomenal activity—a numinous, energetic unfolding from within its own subtle realm--contributes towards archetypal science with the uncovering of its natural self-reflective nature. The revelatory unfolding explored in this hypnopompic encounter supports Jung's archetypal hypothesis that represents epistemological roots of the individuation principle, of "a dynamic potentiality active within the cells of every organism working towards the goal of self-completion" (Card as cited in Stevens, 2002, p. 83), the teleological aspects and transformative effects of which greatly enhances life being lived.

Transpersonal Psychology

Transpersonal psychology has been described as standing at a vital and healing inter-section between science and religion, yet needs to take "one further step to embrace the participatory knowing that all matter is infused with spirit"

working of subtle consciousness is a whole bodily affair, transmitted through multiple inner modes of perceptual knowing. It is not something that can be understood by the power of the intellect alone. When the body is left out, "both the spiritual experience and the unconscious remain disembodied in transpersonal thought" (Louchakova & Lucas, 2007, p. 121). Thus, transpersonal theories can advance through delineating structures of embodied internal perception combined with accounts from living practitioners. First person accounts like mine highlight phenomenological investigation of dream-waking states of consciousness as not only advancing personal consciousness development, but as healing transformative spiritual experiences through which the self is restructured, reorganized and restored (Louchakova & Lucas, 2007, p. 123). Given that all naturally pass from sleeping and/or dreaming into waking consciousness on a daily basis, hypnopompia holds a powerful transformative potential for humanity.

Somatic correlates of psychic events manifest within primitive layers of psyche, and when attention is applied to these process-oriented unfoldings deep within the body, embodied perceptual understanding of powerful energetic forces and metaphysical revelations is generated. This discloses how psychic

> *The regenerative, in-between landscape of dream-waking states suggests, therefore, a much vaster and more complex realm of human perceptions than currently recognized by normative physicalist accounts of embodied awareness.*

(Jaenke, 2004b, p. 14). I hope that the descriptive detail of this hypnopompic experience, that lays bare the subtle, participatory activity and deep healing effect experienced between the realms, can serve to open out this understanding.

Coming to understand the intricate and somatic counterparts interact, and the body as the medium for the expression and realization of being—metaphysical revelations, that do away with older dualistic conceptions that split psyche and soma.

The great divide within the scientific study of consciousness sits between materialistic and nonmaterialistic views of the mind. Hypnopompic revelations help bridge this gap between soma and psyche through bringing forth implicit experiential knowing. When keen observation of these transitional states is intentionally converted into detailed descriptions of psychosomatic processes, which carry heightened sense activation in the proprioceptive and kinesthetic channels, such descriptions provide a refined differentiation of inner-outer energetic unfolding that interacts within the mind-body-spirit continuum.

In times past, transpersonal events such as visionary dream states were recognized as holding enormous value and spiritual purpose, and understood as fundamental aspects of supernatural knowledge, insight and ability (Hollenback, 1996). Yet today, there is a bias against what comes through the visionary imagination … "a form of ethnocentric and logocentric bias that fails to recognize the epistemological legitimacy of more sensory oriented, visual traditions" (Hollenback, 1996). And it is unfortunately still a fact today that science remains unable to deal scientifically with subtle consciousness, continuing to stifle therefore, the advance of psychology as a science (Progroff, 1957/1984). If only it could turn inward, to inner space, to the deep dimensions in the heart of our interiority.

Dream-waking transformative encounters, like the one detailed in this article, offer a third way of experiencing reality, mediated by the depths of the psyche through the body. Hypnopompia offers a way to recover the third middle position, which earlier in western tradition, was the place of soul, "a domain neither physical nor spiritual yet bound to them both" (Hillman, 1975a, p. 68).

It is vitally important then, to learn how to work with and assimilate subtle forms of consciousness that come through dream-waking states, as this leads to fundamental insight into psychic life, thus helping in the development of the faculties of inner life and innate epistemological sources of knowledge.

The in-between hypnopompic state of being is a most subtle state wherein a dynamic process of unfolding perception takes place. This represents "a primary condition for unique types of visionary knowledge" (Irwin, 2015, p. 1). The regenerative, in-between landscape of dream-waking states suggests, therefore, "a much vaster and more complex realm of human perceptions than currently recognized by normative physicalist accounts of embodied awareness" (Irwin, 2015, p. 1).

And so it is high time, or more to the point, well beyond time, the biased blinkers and blinders come off, so the past visionary traditions can be recognized as setting the foundation for the visionaries of the future.

References

A.E. (George William Russell). (1988). Celtic cosmogony. In R & N. Iyer (Eds.). *The descent of the gods: The mystical writings of G.W. Russell—A.E.* (pp. 154–159). Gerrards Cross, UK: Colin Smythe Publishing.

A.E. (George William Russell) (1918). *Candle of Vision: Inner Worlds of the Imagination.* Dublin Ireland: Macmillan Co Press.

Arden, H. (1994). *Dreamkeepers.* New York City, NY: HarperCollins Publishing.

Barrett, D. (2001). *The committee of sleep: How artists, scientists, and athletes use dreams for creative problem solving and how you can too.* New York City, NY: Crown Publishing.

Bhattacharya, S. (2014). "Transcendence of the Time/Space Matrix of Perception iEnlightenment and Near-Death Experience," *Journal for Spiritual & Consciousness Studies,* 37/2: 90-104. Blackmore. (2004). *Consciousness: An introduction.* New York, NY: Oxford University Press.

Carasso, D. (2012). *Religions of mesoamerica.* Long Grove, IL: Waveland Press.

Cressey, J. (1996) Mysticism and the Near Death Experience, In L. Bailey &J. Yates Eds. *The Death Experience: A Reader.* New York: Routledge.

Corbin, H. (1972). *Mundus Imaginalis, the Imaginary and the Imaginal.* Spring, pp. 1–19. NY: Analytical Psychology Club of New York, Inc.

Daly, H. (2016). *Shadowy Beauty: The art of hypnopompic inquiry.* CIIS Doctoral Dissertation. UMI.

Evola, J. (1971). *The hermetic tradition: Symbols, teachings of the royal art.* Rochester, VT: Inner Traditions International.

Faco, E., & Agrillo, Ch. (2012). Near-Death-Like Experiences without Life-Threatening Conditions or Brain Disorders: A Hypothesis from a Case Report. *Frontiers in Psychology,* 3, 490. Doi:/10.3389/fpsyg.2012.0049

Fromm, E. (1957). *The forgotten language: An introduction to the understanding of dreams, fairytales and myths.* New York City, NY: Grove Press, Inc. (Original work published, 1951)

Garcia-Romeu, A.P. (2010). Self-transcendence as a measurable transpersonal construct. *Journal of Transpersonal Psychology,* 42(1), 26-47.

Garcia-Romeu, A.P., & Tart. C. (2013). Altered States of Consciousness. In H. L. Friedman & G. Hartelius (Eds.). *The Wiley-Blackwell Handbook of Transpersonal Psychology,* pp. 121- 139, John Wiley & Sons, Ltd.

Garrett, E. (1943). *Awareness.* Greenport, NY: Parapsychology Foundation Inc.

Gertz, J. (1983). Hypnagogic fantasy, EEG, and psi performance in a single subject. *Journal of the American Society for Psychical Research,* 77. 155-170.

Greyson, B. (2000). Near-Death Experiences. In E. Cardena, S. J. Lynn, & S. Krippner (Eds), *Varieties of anomalous experience: Examining the scientific evidence,* pp. 315-352. Washington, DC: American Psychological Association.

Grosso, M. (1996). Archetype of Death and Enlightenment: In L.W. Bailey & Yates, J. L. Yates (Ed.). *The near-death experience: A Reader,* New York: Routledge

Grosso, M. (1994). The status of survival research: Evidence, problems, paradigms. *Noetic Sciences Review,* 32, 12-20.

Heidegger, M. *(1926). Being and time. Oxford, UK: Routledge.*

Heron, J., & Reason, P. (1997). A participatory inquiry paradigm. *Qualitative Inquiry,* 3, 274–294. Doi/10.1177/107780049700300302

Hillman, J. (1975a). Loose ends: *Primary papers in archetypal psychology.* Thompson, CT: Spring Publications.

Hillman, J. (1979). *The dream and the underworld.* New York, NY: Harper and Row Publishing.

Hollenback, J. (1996). *Mysticism: Experience, Response, and Empowerment,* University Park: The Pennsylvania State University Press, 8-16.

Irwin, L. (1994). *The dream seekers: Native American visionary tradition of the great plains,* Norman OK: University of Oklahoma Press.

Irwin, L. (1994). On Lucid Dreaming: Memory, Meaning, and Imagination. In R. Hurd and K. Bulkeley (Eds) *Lucid Dreaming: New Perspectives on Consciousness in Sleep:* Two Volumes. Berkeley, CA: Praeger, 1. pp. 103-126.

Irwin, L. (2015). Mystical knowledge and near death experience. In C. Moreman & T. Cattoi (Ed.), *Death, dying, and mysticism* (pp. 153–175). Basinstoke, UK: Palgrave.

Jaenke, K. (2004). Ode to the Intelligence of Dreams, *Revision: Journal of Consciousness and Transformation,* Vol. 27, (1), 2-8. Doi: 10.3200/revn.27.1.2-48

Jaenke, K. (2004b). The participatory turn: Review of Jorge N. Ferrer, Revisioning transpersonal theory: A participatory vision of human spirituality. *Revision: A Journal of Consciousness and Transformation,* 26(4), 8-14.

James, W. (1990). *Varieties of Religious Experience: A Study in Human Nature,* NY: Vintage Books/Library of America.

Jung, C. G. (1933). *Modern man in search of a soul.* Orlando, FL: Houghton Mifflin Harcourt Publishing Company.

Jung, C. G. (1964). *Man and his symbols.* New York City, NY: Dell Publishing, Random House, Inc.

Jung, C. G. (1974). Dreams. In G. Adler (Ed.) & R. Hull (Trans.). *The collected works of C.G Jung* (Vol. 18). Princeton, NJ: Princeton University Press.

Jung, C. G. (1983). Alchemical Studies. In G. Adler (Ed.) & R. Hull, (Trans.). *The collected works of C.G. Jung* (Vol. 13) Princeton, NJ: Princeton University Press.

Kearney, R. (1998). *Poetics of imaging: Modern and post-modern* (Perspectives in continental philosophy). Bronx, NY: Fordham University Press.

Keen, S. (1974). *Voices and visions.* New York City, NY: Harper and Row Publishers.

Lachman, G. (2002). Waking sleep: The hypnopompic state. *Fortean Times.* Retrieved from: http://forteantimes.com

Lachman, G. (2009). *Swedenborg: An introduction to his life and ideas.* Westminister, UK: Penguin Publishing Group.

Laughlin, C. D., McManus, J., & E.G. d'Aquili (1990). *Brain, symbol and experience: Toward a neurophenomenology of human consciousness.* Boston, MA: Shambhala.

Leroy, E.B. (1933). *Les Visions du demi-sommeil.* Paris: Librarie Felix Alcan, (Original work published 1926).

Levin, D. (1985/2003). *The body's recollection of being.* Oxford, UK: Routledge. (Original work published 1985).

Levin, J., & Steel, L. (2005). The transcendent experience: Conceptual, theoretical, and epidemiological perspectives. *Explore,* 1(2), 89-101. Doi:10/1016/j.explore.2004.12.002

Louchakova, O., & Lucas, M. K. (1997). Transpersonal self as a clinical category: Reflections on culture, gender, and phenomenology. *The Journal of Transpersonal Psychology,* 39(2),111–127.

Matthews, C. (1989). *The elements of the Celtic tradition.* Dorset, UK: Element Books Limited.

Mavromatis, A. (2010). *Hypnopompia: The unique state of consciousness between wakefulness and sleep.* London, UK: Thyrsos Press.

Meier, C.A. (1986). *Soul and body: Essays on the theories of Jung.* Culver City, CA: Lapis Press.

Meier, C. A. (1989). *Healing, dream, and ritual.* Switzerland: Daimon Verlag Publishing.

Merleau-Ponty, M. (2006). *Phenomenology of perception.* New York City: Routledge.

Metzner, R. (1998). *The unfolding self.* Novato, CA: Origin Press.

McKeller, P. (1957). *Imagination and thinking; A psychological analysis.* London: Cohen & West

Moody, M. (1975). *Life after life.* New York City, NY: Bantam Books.

Neumann, E. (1974). *The great mother: An analysis of the archeytype.* Princeton, N.J: Princeton University Press.

Northrop, F. (1966). *Blake: A collection of critical essays, New Jersey:* Prentice-Hall Publishing.

Osbon, D. K. (1991). *Reflections on the art of living: A Joseph Campbell companion.* New York, NY: HarperCollins Publishing.

Otto, R. (1958). The idea of the holy. Oxford, UK: Oxford University Press. (Original work published 1923)

Ouspensky, P. D. (1974). The Psychology of man's possible evolution. NY: Vintage Books.

Peat, D. (2005). *Blackfoot physics.* Newburyport, MA: Weiser Books.

Perera, S. B. (1981). *Descent to the Goddess: A way of initiation for women.* Toronto, Canada: Inner City Books.

Perera, S. B., & Whitmont, E. C. (1996). *Dreams: A portal to the source.* Oxford, UK: Routledge Publishing.

Powell, A. J. (2018). *Mind and Spirit: hypnagogia and religious experience.* Retrieved from http://www.thelancet.com/psychiatry

Progroff, I. (1984). *The cloud of unknowing.* Alexandra, VA: Julian Press. (Original work published 1957).

Ring, K. & Valarino, E. (1998). *Lessons from the light,* New York City, NY: MacMillan Publishing.

Ring, K. (2006). *Lessons from the Light: What we can learn from near death experience,* Needham: Moment Point Press, 285-300 (Original work published 1998)

Sechrist, E. (1968). *Dreams: Your logic mirror, with interpretations of Edgar Cayce.* New York City, NY: Cowles Education Corporation.

Schacter, D. L. (1976). The hypnagogic state: A critical review of the literature. *Psychological Bulletin.* 83. pp. 452-481. Doi:/10.1037/0033-2909.83.3.452

Shafton, A. (1995). *Contemporary approaches to the understanding of dreams.* Albany, NY: State University of New York Press.

Sheldrake, P. (1995). *Living between two worlds, place and journey in Celtic spirituality.* Cambridge: MA. Cowley Publications.

Sherwood, S. (2002). Relationship between the hypnagogic/hypnopompic states and reports of anomalous experiences. *The Journal of Parapsychology.* Vol 66, (2) pp. 127-152.

Silberer, H. (1965). Report on a method of eliciting and observing certain symbolic hallucination-phenomena. In Rapaport, D. (Ed) *Organization and Pathology of Thought.* New York: Columbia University Press, 1965. (Original work published in 1917).

Smith, H. (1992). *Forgotten truth: The common vision of the world's religion,* New York City, NY: HarperCollins Publishing.

Stevens, A. (2002). *Archetype revisited: An updated natural history of the self.* Toronto, Ontario: Inner City Books.

Stewart, R. J. (1992). *The power in the land: The roots of Celtic and underworld tradition,* Dorset, UK: Element Books Limited.

Sellars, J. (2018). Transpersonal and Transformative Potential of Out-of-Body Experiences, *Journal of Exceptional Experiences and Psychology,* Vol 6 (2), pp. 7-27.

Stumbrys, T. (2018), Bridging Lucid Dream Research and Transpersonal Psychology: Toward Transpersonal Studies of Lucid Dreams. *The Journal of Transpersonal Psychology,* Vol.50,No. 2

Tart, C. (1975). *States of consciousness.* Westminister, UK: E.P. Dutton & Co., Inc.

Tart, C. (1997). *Body, mind, spirit: Exploring the parapsychology of spirituality.* Newburyport, MA: Hampton Roads Publishing Company, Inc.

Taylor, T. (1984). *On the mysteries: Iamblichus.* San Diego, CA: Wizards Publishers.

von Franz, M.L. (1998). *On dreams and death: A Jungian interpretation* (E.X. Kennedy & V Brooks, Trans.). Boston, MA: Shambala Publications.

Waters, F. et al (2016). What is the Link Between Hallucinations, Dreams, and Hypnagogic-Hypnopompic Experiences. *Schizophrenia Bulletin.* Vol 42, no 5, pp. 1098-1109, Doi: 10.1093/schbul/sbw076.

Wedemeyer, C. (2010). *Hermeneutics, politics, and history of religions.* Oxford, UK: Oxford Publishing Press.

Whitehead. C. (2011). Altered consciousness in society. In E. Cardena & M. Winkelman (Eds.) *Altering consciousness: Multidisciplinary perspectives, Vol 1, History, culture and the humanities, pp. 181-202.* Santa Barbara, CA: Praeger.

Whelan, D. (2010). Ever ancient, ever new: *Celtic spirituality in the 21st century.* Dublin, Ireland: Original Writing Limited.

The Quest

Into altered states

Into sickness

Into emptiness

   I followed you

Across the border

Through deep water

Above timberline

   I followed you

Into lovers' arms

   I followed you

Into great libraries

   I followed you

Into monasteries

   I followed you

Everywhere you went

   I followed you

Until you returned.

—*Meredith Sabini*

University for Peace

Created by the United Nations General Assembly in 1980, the University for Peace trains future leaders to explore and formulate strategies and practices to address the causes of problems affecting human and global wellbeing.

The MA and PhD Degree in Indigenous Science and Peace Studies (ISPS)

This program examines the traditions of Indigenous peoples of the world and their generations-tested ways of making peace and balancing societies, offering a roadmap to prosperity that respects individual and collective rights, local development models and environmental solutions.

IS IT FOR YOU?

Do you want to help solve the global crises facing humanity by transforming outdated paradigms?

Are you inspired to learn how Indigenous knowledge and Western science can be employed across disciplines and professions to transform crises and conflicts, and build peace?

Do you want to spend a year studying in an academically challenging environment, at a global university with students, faculty, and Indigenous Elders from around the world?

WHAT WILL YOU LEARN?

Steeped in Indigenous Knowledge Systems and methodologies, the MA or PhD Degree in Indigenous Science and Peace Studies (ISPS) will train you to be an insightful researcher and practitioner who understands the central issues that impact diplomacy, policymaking, and community work.

- Learn a synthesis of indigenous scientific research and theory relevant to the transformation of conflicts.
- Gain a diversity of perspectives that impact peace, justice, security, sovereignty, and reconciliation.
- Obtain detailed knowledge of the United Nations System and related institutions, procedures and instruments that affect decision-making regarding Indigenous peoples and traditional knowledge.

This course enables students to become more effective policymakers, community workers, diplomats, activists, and communicators who create change to renew life on earth.

**For more information, go to www.upeace.org/programmes/indigenous-science-and-peace.
To apply, go to www.upeace.org/pages/apply-admission.**

The main campus of the University for Peace is located in San Jose, Costa Rica

Expansion and Contraction in the Dreaming Body

Karen Jaenke, PhD

This article explores psycho-somatic states of expansion and contraction awakened by dreams, along with methods for consciously engaging with hypnopompic states in order to resolve the constrictions of trauma in favor of spaciousness.

First, it looks at several dreams of the author that confer expansive states. These dreams reveal that affect joy accompanies states of expansiveness in the subtle body.

Secondly, the article considers what disrupts and interferes with the human experience of joy, focusing on trauma. Experiences of trauma involving the freeze response impinge on our sense of spaciousness, resulting in fragmentation and constriction in the body-psyche, which is the antithesis of joy. With their healing impetus, dreams surface imagery

Photos:
p. 35 Hubble Space Telescope, courtesy NASA.
p. 38 Tree of Light, painting, Karen Jaenke.
All others: Karen Jaenke

depicting contracted states—dense and disturbing images to encounter and metabolize.

However, a meditative practice of meeting zones of contraction in the body-psyche with mindful awareness allows contraction to relax into spaciousness. By developing the robust mindfulness that is necessary to meet sites of extreme density in the body, trauma's contraction is released into joyous expansion.

Literature Review

A brief review of the literature on somatic approaches to dreams provides a contextual framework for this exploration. First, I consider foundational tenets supplied by Joseph Campbell on the relationship of body anatomy to imagination, myths and dreams. Then, four somatic approaches to dreams are examined: Arnold Mindell's dreambody approach of attending to channels and processes in the body to resolve symptoms; Eugene Gendlin's focusing, felt sense and growth-direction approach; Robert Boznak's embodiment method of anchoring dream images in the body; and Karen Jaenke's hypnopomic approach to the somatic understructure of dreams.

In *The Power of Myth* (1988), 20th century mythologist Joseph Campbell emphasizes the bodily foundations that underlie imagination, dreams and myths. For Campbell the deepest source and framework for imagination is located in the anatomical organization of the human body. "The imagination is grounded in the energy of the organs of the body, and these are the same in all human beings. Since imagination comes out of one biological ground, it is bound to produce certain themes" (Campbell, 1988, p. 42). Moreover, according to Campbell, myths and dreams are storied depictions of the struggles, conflicts and potentials found within the body:

> Dreams are manifestations in image form of the energies of the body in conflict with each other.... Myth is a manifestation in symbolic images, in metaphorical images, of the energies of the organs of the body in conflict with each other. This organ wants this, that organ wants that. The brain is one of the organs (1988, p. 39).

Karen Jaenke, PhD Served as Chair of the Consciousness & Transformative Studies Masters degree program at National University (formerly John F. Kennedy University) from 2013 to 2022. In 2016, she launched and built the online modality for the Consciousness & Transformative Studies program, giving this cutting-edge program global reach. In 2021, she added to this leading-edge curriculum a Coach Training Program certified by the International Coaching Federation. Formerly, she served as Director of the Ecotherapy Certificate Program at JFKU (2011-14) and Dissertation Director at the Institute of Imaginal Studies in Petaluma, CA (2001-2008). An Executive Editor of ReVision: Journal of Consciousness and Transformation, she has edited journals and published articles on the topics of Imaginal Psychology, Shamanism and the Wounded West, Earth Dreaming, and Places of Hope, as well as numerous articles on dreams and consciousness. A repeat presenter at the International Association for the Study of Dreams, Society for the Study of Shamanism, and Science and Nonduality conferences, her creative vision synthesizes dreamwork, indigenous ways of knowing, subtle body awareness, living systems theory, and flow states.

Similarly, noting a connection between dreams and body symptoms, Arnold Mindell (2002) coined the term *dreambody*, defined as "a multi-channeled information sender asking you to receive its message in many ways and notice how its information appears over and over again in dreams and body symptoms" (2002, p. 33). Following Freud (1953), Mindell differentiates between primary processes, those closer to awareness, including content that one can verbalize and consciously direct, and secondary processes, which are unconscious phenomena, like body symptoms and dreams, of which one is only vaguely aware and unable to control. Yet by discovering an unfolding psycho-somatic process, and amplifying its channel, Mindell discovered a symptom can turn into healing. His dreambody approach is highly specific to the individual situation and unpredictable, similar to the processes of nature.

Mindell's dreambody work (2002) takes Jung's practice of active imagination (1960), or consciously engaging with the impulses and images of one's unconscious, and broadens it into a multi-channeled exploration. Mindell differentiates several different channels through which dreams and body processes seek to communicate information: the visual, auditory, kinesthetic, proprioceptive, and world channels. The first four of these refer to seeing, hearing, moving, and sensing/feeling, while the last refers to outer events that grab our attention. The proprioceptive channel refers to body awareness, namely, sensing and feeling the messages and sensations occurring inside the body, such as pain, tightness, cramping, pressure, blockage, constriction, or tingling.

In *Let Your Body Interpret Your Dreams* (1986), Eugene Gendlin applies his focusing method to dreams, encouraging dreamers to adopt a welcoming attitude towards the inchoate, nonverbal "felt sense" that often accompanies dreams, putting one's attention on the "felt sense," and seeing where the energy wants to move, where it opens, expands, or releases. Gendlin defines the "felt sense" in this way:

> A felt sense is not a mental experience but a physical one. *Physical*. A bodily awareness of a situation or person or event. An internal aura that encompasses everything you feel and know about the given subject at a given time—encompasses it and communicates it to you all at once rather than detail by detail (1981, p. 32).

I was first initiated into the paradox of spacious awareness through several dreams in which death played a prominent role; experiences of overflowing spacious joy accompanied this death imagery.

The felt sense is meaningful, though the meaning is initially unknown, so this practice requires an ability to suspend rational knowing, in favor of trusting an emergent process within the body. The "felt sense" offers vital clues to a "growth-direction," incremental shifts seeking to emerge from within the body and the dream. This inner stirring is how life-energy feels when it organically moves forward. When a pro-life, forward-moving growth process is active, energy flows, bringing a sense of expansive spaciousness and inner guidance. The expansive movement in the body acts as a guide, confirming this little step or shift in awareness is in the right direction, i.e., in the direction of vitality. Conversely, mental resistance to the life energy brings constriction, tightness and narrowing. With practice, one learns to differentiate the expansive, life-enhancing growth direction, from blocked places where there is life-limitation, opposition, and constriction. Inherent in Gendlin's approach is a profound trust in the deep guiding wisdom of the body. Implicitly, then, Gendlin's method applies nonverbal

somatic awareness to the dream discernment process, as a primary indication of the emerging growth possibilities of personhood.

Robert Bosnak (2007) offers another somatic approach to dreams known as embodiment, defining *embodied images* with the help of recent dream and sleep brain research. Following Hobson (2002), he agrees that emotion is a primary shaper of dream plots. Following Solms (2000), he found that the part of the brain activated during dreaming is a region that spatially organizes information. Bosnak defines embodied images as "surrounding, imagined, quasi-physical environments and presences in and among which we find ourselves, presenting themselves as self-evidently real, accompanied by basic physiological processes" (2007, p. 41).

Embodiment is a type of dreamwork in which the affects and sensations associated with dream images are anchored in the body and then experienced simultaneously. The dreamer is facilitated to re-experience the dream, slowly and methodically in a frame-by-frame manner that reveals specific image-feeling-sensations. Adopting dual consciousness, simultaneously in waking consciousness verbalizing one's experience while experiencing the dream environment, the dreamer's awareness is brought to the details of the image environment, including affective states and physical sensations. When the affect is being fully experienced, the dreamer is asked to locate it in the body. After fully embodying the affective states and physical sensations together, the dreamer is guided towards another dream image, until the most significant dream images are anchored in the body.

Finally, by experiencing the various dream images simultaneously, along with their affective and somatic aspects, the dream is metabolized systemically, as a single simultaneous system, allowing for the psycho-somatic energy behind the dream to be gathered and cohered, then re-organized. This process "releases the static energy, clogged in dissociated isolation, into a larger system as a quickening fresh circulation" (2007, p 134).

In "Ode to the Intelligence of Dreams," Karen Jaenke (2004) advocates applying Gendlin's felt sense method during hypnopompia, the transitional state between sleeping and waking, while the dream is fresh and the dreamer remains in an altered state of consciousness. The conditions of hypnopompia offer "a vast gold mine for deep exploration of a cellular, bodily, ancestral kind of knowing" (2004, p. 8-9). Hypnopompia entails "a transition point in consciousness where there is a vortex or opening to enter the somatic underbelly of the dream, the place that the dream images are literally born and carried in the flesh" (Jaenke, 2004, p. 8). Building on Gendlin's method, she finds that dreams: arise along the psycho-somatic interface; carry not only the well-known visual and verbal dimensions but also visceral dimensions; possess a somatic understructure, appearing in the body or subtle body in a particular configuration; constitute the body's speech in image form; provide access to cellular memory deposits; hold their interpretive meaning in the body, in the precise corporeal way that the dream appears; possess a form of "intelligence built on the foundation of sensation"; and ultimately drive at "a completely awakened body… and vitalized person" (Jaenke, 2004, p. 9).

Through a practice of deep sensory awareness during the hypnopompic state, the attentive mind is carried into deep and unknown caverns of cellular memory and somatic awareness, into a primal knowing. [The] return to an archaic way of knowing…[transmits] contact with the primitive igniting spark of the life force. This descent into primeval origins, into an archaic awareness of a primordial animating force, quickens and refreshes the tired stasis of the (post)modern mind. It

> *Upon waking, floating in the in-between space between dreaming and waking—I am flooded with pure bliss.*

has the potential to counterbalance and heal the dominant evolutionary direction of human culture… an ever-increasing dissociation from nature (Jaenke, 2004, p. 9).

Expansive States in Dreams

Applying Gendlin's sensory awareness method, this article seeks to explore states of expansion and contraction that appear in conjunction with dreams, accessed during the hypnopompic state of awakening through mindfulness. For each of us, dreams impart a natural, nightly, and direct expression from the depths of the psyche. Indeed, dreams arguably present the most direct and transparent voice of the soul regularly available to us.

The language of dreams is images. Dream images are often accompanied by intensified affects and bodily sensations, as well as perceptive insights into the dreamer's life situation and the human condition. In addition, dreams bear both a retrospective function, assisting in gathering a more complete personal and collective memory, and a prospective function, with hints and openings to higher developmental potentials. Due to this prospective function, dreams can awaken previously unimagined expansive states of being.

Expansion in Death Dreams: A Personal Example

My most stunning and lucid states of expansive consciousness appeared in dreams. Notably, these expansive dream states were accompanied by the affect joy. The imagery of these joy-filled dreams coalesces into two types, which, at first glance, may appear startling—imagery associated with death, and imagery associated with physical matter. This surprising imagery hints at the paradoxical nature of expansive states and of joy.

I was first initiated into the paradox of spacious awareness through several dreams in which death played a prominent role; experiences of overflowing spacious joy accompanied this death imagery. The most striking of these death-joy dreams occurred while I was taking an intensive graduate course on Death and Dying in summer 1995, with an immersion, day and night, in readings, conversations, and musings on death. A few years earlier, I regularly encountered with death while working as a prison chaplain in an AIDS unit in the late 1980s. With no cure for this stigmatized and feared disease, men close to my own age, 30, were dying all around me from AIDS, moreover without

any ability to fulfill a single final wish, due to their incarceration. Simultaneously, I visited the sole woman on death row in the state of New Jersey, who was facing a radically different type of death, ominous and foreboding, with even greater social stigma. With a little distance from the immediacy of these experiences, I welcomed the opportunity to explore death from an academic perspective

A few days after completing my final paper for the class, the following dream appeared:

A former professor of mine, an elder whom I held in high esteem, and his wife, also a cherished friend, have just died. I am at their house, [where I had previously house-sat for two summers], along with their four children, who are sorting through their belongings. While at the house, Gib, my former professor, calls on the phone from Death. We talk for a few minutes, before I finally gather the courage to ask him what it is like where he is. After a poignant pause, he confides, "Oh,

> ...joy dwells at the boundary where the opposites, life and death, meet and merge into one another.

Karen, it is the most wonderful thing. From here, I can see that at the core of all reality is bliss." As he speaks, waves of pure bliss fill me, as if transmitted on the wings of his words. I enter a state of complete expansiveness, from which all boundaries, tensions, and fears are banished – I am one with all that is, without separations and contractions. It is the most complete and full state of being ever known to me.

> Dreams of death often signify deep transformative processes at work.

Upon waking, floating in the in-between space between dreaming and waking—I am flooded with pure bliss. There is a vast opening into lucid awareness and spacious stillness. Gradually, this dissolves into reflective attention towards the subtle energies unleashed by the dream. Then comes a gradual falling away from the seamless expansiveness, descending through layers of reality, contracting at each layer, as I come back into awareness of my body, and my normal personality is re-constituted.

The contraction brings unimaginable anguish, tempered, however, by the consolation of having just glimpsed and partaken of ultimate reality. The epiphany being so utterly perfect, a secondary knowing suggests that an entire lifetime may be required to realize, inhabit, and embody this perfection of joy. I glimpse a possibility I did not know existed, and my soul's desire to consciously cultivate spaciousness and joy has just been awakened.

Subsequent dreams similarly coupled images of death with states of profound expansiveness and joy, indicating that joy is intimately bound, not only to profound ego-death, and utter submission to the ultimate mystery of death, but also that joy dwells at the boundary where the opposites, life and death, meet and merge into one another. The life-death polarity represents perhaps the most profound archetypal reality to be encountered; and at the synergistic place of their meeting, joy abounds.

Dreams of death often signify deep transformative processes at work. Death dreams may also offer windows or glimpses into other dimensions of reality. Dreams of death often usher in archetypal realms charged with numinous energies, challenging us to expand our capacity to experience and assimilate the most intense human emotions. Death dreams may challenge our conceptual and intellectual frameworks by expanding our notions of the real and the possible, transporting us to dimensions of experience and reality outside typical belief systems. Integrating such reality-shattering dreams may require deconstruction of prior worldviews and creation of new, vastly expanded frameworks or cosmology. Finally, death dreams may transport us into dimensions of reality designated as spiritual, radiating a sacred quality, bearing the presence of the numinous, eliciting utmost respect and reverence, inspiring "sacred emotions" of holy terror, solemn awe, as well as states of ultimate consolation, joy, and bliss.

Expansion in Dreams of Matter: A Personal Example

In addition to death as the harbinger of spaciousness, in my experience, a second distinct type of dream imagery accompanies vastly expansive states of consciousness, perhaps still more surprising and mysterious. These dreams concern matter—yes, material reality, all along its continuum from dense to subtle. Since these dreams depict transformations between matter and energy, dynamics of expansion and contraction, and the continuum from dense to subtle reality, the worldview and metaphors of quantum physics become pertinent.

The first of these "matter dreams" penetrates into the mystery behind the most dense form of matter encountered in our everyday lives, the stones. This dream appeared near the culmination of a group pilgrimage to the Arctic Circle region in summer 1997, during a cultural exchange with the Saami people, the last remaining indigenous peoples of Northern Europe. On the morning our group was to make the trek to an ancient, rock-carving site, the following dream synchronistically appeared:

Walking alone in thick woods, I find myself enmeshed in a thick tangle of branches, leaves, trunks, and vines, knotted together into a dense forest. Everything is cloaked in shades of gray: branches, vines, roots and undergrowth weave together into one intertwined mesh of gray. Making my way through the dense thicket, I notice something that stands apart from the vegetation—a tall standing stone. Angling towards it, I see a series of tall standing stones extending off to my left, dwarfing me. Rising in the shape of solid arches, the large gray boulders appear like grand hooded beings. Huge gray stones people the forest! Then suddenly I realize the stones are alive with energy—energy more immense and all-pervasive than any

> A veil has been pulled back, the immense energy present in matter, $E=mc^2$, has suddenly exploded from behind the appearance of solidity, unleashed in the room, in my body, in both all at once.

I've ever known. They are living beings just like me!

I awaken awash in a sea of energy. The surrounding space dances with motion. A mysterious vibration emanates equally everywhere, without beginning or end, source or direction. Within this electrified space, no discrete thing stands apart with its own form—there is only one continuous field, supercharged with pulsation. Boundaries of discrete things give way to fluid motion. Unceasing waves of energy envelop me. Quivering vibration is all that I know.

Suspended, my mind circles round one shifting impression and then another. *This is matter and vibration—I swim here. Energy is everywhere and I float in it.* A veil has been pulled back, the immense energy present in matter, $E=mc^2$, has suddenly exploded from behind the appearance of solidity, unleashed in the room, in my body, in both all at once. *So this is the energy of the stones, and they are alive!* I awaken to the epiphany of my elemental kinship with the stones.

The living stones pummel me with energy more vitally alive than anything I have ever known! My electrified consciousness expands into the surrounding space, knowing no boundaries, losing all sense of self and non-self. Awareness of reality as one shimmering expanse of vibration, and the transparency of my participation within it, bestows effervescent joy.

These dramatic somatic shifts, occurring in the immediate aftermath of the dream—impart a wholly new sense of embodiment, as a light body composed of pure energy, with no solidity whatsoever. In addition, the stunning aliveness challenges the plodding density of my thought patterns, presenting a radically new vision of reality—as a seamless field of pure energy. The worldview of the dream is akin to that of quantum physics, attesting that all matter is in fact energy, arranged according to different degrees of density.

Expansion in Dreams of Death and Matter: A Personal Example

While this dream reveals the superabundance of energy, vitality and joy present in the densest concentrations of matter naturally occurring on earth, a subsequent dream in winter 2001 exposes the mystery of matter at the opposite end of the continuum. It deposits me inside the life force of a single particle, traveling at the far edge of the universe, where new space is being unfurled. Transcending time and space, the dream reaches across a continuum as vast as the universe itself. Once again, death is the doorway into this expansive state:

My beloved grandmother, my precious dog and I stand together at a precarious three-way intersection near my house. Suddenly a red vehicle races towards us at top speed, and for a split nano-second, I know everything is about to change. Yet there is no time to act. The three of us are hit and thrown to the other side. We lose track of one another, and I find myself on a solitary journey travelling through space.

Disoriented, tumbling in space, I seek to find my bearings in this unfamiliar dimension of reality. I realize that here reality is composed of vortices or cones, narrow at one end and wide at the other. The only choice available to me is which way to orient within this vortex. I choose to orient towards the expansive direction, psychically gravitating towards greater expansiveness. Then I come to the expansive end of this vortex, only to discover that the wide end of the first vortex is the narrow end of the next vortex. Again, I am presented with the same choice—to go either narrow or wide, to constrict or expand. And again, I choose to orient towards the expansive direction. Then once again, the wide end of the second vortex becomes the narrow end of the next vortex. Again, I choose expansiveness.

This scenario repeats several times. Each time reaffirming my choice for expansion, finally I am carried as a solitary particle to the far edge of the universe, where new space itself is being created. At the far frontier of the cosmos, I travel as a light body across vast expanses, where matter exists in its least dense form, where single particles journey

in unfathomable spaciousness. Participation in this unfurling of new space, spatiating as a light body particle, bestows ineffable freedom, lightness of being, bliss.

Upon awaking from this dream, my consciousness gradually reverses direction, passing back through successive degrees of contraction, from the most subtle to the more dense, until finally arriving at the familiar density that accompanies my normal self-awareness and recognizable personality.

The passage through death in the dream, along with revelation of out-of-this-world expansiveness on the other side, left me feeling quite tentative in life. For several weeks afterwards, there was an inescapable impression that physical death was coming. Entering such an otherworldly place of freedom, expansion, and bliss, it did not seem possible that my life could continue on. The dream must be a premonition, even preparation, for death. Yet after several weeks passed and death did not come, it dawned on me that instead the dream had imparted the task of remaining in life while realizing this utmost spaciousness in this lifetime, in this world, within the constraints of my physical existence.

This extraordinary passage—traversing the cosmic distance from embodiment as dense physical matter to ultimate weightlessness and light, then back again—is also found in various spiritual traditions. The teachings of the Gnostics, for instance, convey a perception of how spirit becomes matter, as a movement from a subtle dimension into dense form. From this perspective, the process of incarnation, of taking on a body, entails a condensation or contraction from the light body of the spirit world, into the denser forms of embodiment found in our physical world. The incarnation process, going from the invisible spirit world into physical existence, necessitates a severe compression, a movement into great density, relative to the lightness of the spirit world, our original and final home.

The particle dream reveals the exquisite joy and freedom of the single particle, loosed from all bondage to other matter, thereby linking human bliss to ultimate spaciousness. Moreover, the dream transmits an experience that extends across the full spectrum of reality—from dense to

> *The living stones pummel me with energy more vitally alive than anything I have ever known.*

subtle and back again. My consciousness traverses this entire continuum—from embodiment as a single particle at the far edge of the universe, where empty space is greatest —to the concentrated embodiment of a human body dwelling upon earth.

When paired with the stones dream, taken together, the two dreams—of dense stones and single particle—herald the possibilities of expansiveness across the entire continuum of matter, and from Earth across the far-flung expanses of the universe. Boundaryless spaciousness is revealed as equally present in the tightly compressed rock, and in the tiniest speck of matter at the farthest reaches of the cosmos. Together these two dreams reveal the most marvelous truth: that across the entire continuum of reality, from dense to

> *Transcending time and space, the dream reaches across a continuum as vast as the universe itself. Once again, death is the doorway into this expansive state.*

subtle, the possibilities of expansive consciousness remain ever present. Spacious awareness exists in potentia throughout the entire extension of the cosmos, vibrating within the heartbeat of all forms and appearances. "At the core of all reality is bliss!

States of Contraction in Trauma

If spacious awareness is present as a living potential across the entire continuum of the cosmos, why is it so challenging for human beings access and sustain expansive states of joy? And how can human beings, in their specifically human form—more compact and dense than the particle yet less densely concentrated than the stones—cultivate their own share in the cosmic joy potential deposited throughout creation?

The primary challenge for our species in participating in the greater joy of the cosmos is the reality of trauma. Trauma entails an experience of overwhelm, due to the impingement of other forces upon one's own life force, which threatens the viability or vitality of one's own existence. Etymologically, the word *trauma*, coming from Greek, means 'wound'.

Since no one has long been in this world without encountering threats by other forces, in varying degrees, trauma is a reality we all must contend with in the quest for spaciousness and joy. Given the ubiquity of threatening forces, evolution equipped us with automatic mechanisms to respond to these vital threats. However, while our programmed response to immediate danger—fight, flight or freeze—helps us survive in a world that poses risks to our survival, it can also impede our participation in expansive states of consciousness.

Since trauma is a prime factor hindering our participation in expansive states of being, understanding our biological programming in response to danger and trauma is paradoxically relevant to the exploration of joy and expansive states of being. A short detour into the underlying dynamics of trauma reveals how the trauma response results in fragmentation and constriction, both of which are antithetical to the experience of spaciousness and joy.

The four components of trauma are: hyperarousal, constriction, dissociation, and freezing/immobility (Levine, 1997, p. 132). Helplessness is associated with the freeze response. In abject helplessness, immobilization and paralysis take over, preventing one from screaming, moving, or feeling (Levine, 1997, p. 142). None of these responses are under our voluntary control, but rather are embedded in our biological programming, occurring automatically, often outside conscious awareness.

When external forces impinge in a potentially life-threatening way, and danger is perceived, the initial response is typically shock; meanwhile the nervous system instinctively mobilizes tremendous resources to fight the threat through heightened arousal, energizing our survival mechanisms to meet the challenge. "The amount of energy mobilized [in a vital threat] is much higher than that mobilized for any other situation in our lives" (Levine, 1997, p. 133). Subsequently, when this energy is not discharged through the action of either fighting or fleeing, it becomes backed up in the nervous system. Trauma symptoms then arise "as short-term solutions to the dilemma of undischarged energy" (Levine, 1997, p. 134).

The fight and flight responses, if successfully executed, tend not to result in psychological trauma, for the tremendous energy mobilized through the physiology of alarm and adrenaline surge become discharged through the act of fighting or fleeing. However, if neither fight nor flight is possible, due to overpowering threat or the developmental limitations of immaturity (as in a fetus, infant or child), the freeze option remains the only recourse. When freezing occurs, the tremendous somatic energies aroused and mobilized for fight or flight are not discharged, but instead become dammed up in the nervous system, later generating energetic and emotional disturbances.[1]

The constriction of attention that typically occurs in threatening situations heightens one's ability to focus on the threat and act in a maximally optimal way. When constriction fails as a sufficient strategy for mobilizing self-defense, the nervous system adopts the last resort, freezing and dissociation, as a means to channel the tremendous energies and overwhelming emotions of the hyper-aroused state.

Psychologically speaking, trauma entails an experience of extreme overwhelm; trauma assaults and overwhelms

> …trauma assaults and overwhelms the processing centers of experience. The person is unable to digest the full experience in the moment it occurs.

the processing centers of experience. The person is unable to digest the full experience in the moment it occurs. The normal mode of processing experience is intercepted by the shock response, and the traumatic event is automatically compartmentalized and set aside, i.e. suppressed or repressed, for later tending. This dramatic interruption in the flow of experience, known as dissociation, enables a person to endure experiences that in the moment are beyond endurance, serving a valuable survival function to keep the overwhelming emotions and undischarged energy of hyperarousal outside of conscious awareness. Dissociation refers to a breakdown in the continuity of a person's felt sense, or bodily awareness.

In the detaching of awareness from the body, the mind is employed "not to discover facts but to hide them" (Damasio, 1999, p. 28). What gets hidden is the body and its interiority. "Like a veil…, the screen partially removes from the mind the inner states of the body, those that constitute the flow of life" (Damasio, 1999, p. 28).

Dissociation severs the organic wholeness of experience, in various critical ways: a disconnection can occur between consciousness and the body; between one part of the body and the rest of the body; between awareness and emotions, thoughts and sensations; or between awareness and the memory of part or all of the threatening event (Levine, 1997, p. 140). Thus heavily traumatized individuals lose the ability to attend to their inner sensations and perceptions (Van der Kolk, 2006, p. 11). Hence the constituent elements of experience—cognition, affect, sensation and image—that under normal circumstances are held together cohesively and processed as a single unit, become fractured by overwhelming trauma.

However, the mechanism of dissociation serves to enable the psychological system to handle the state of overload—by fragmenting experience, dividing up and parceling out the totality of the trauma event into separate parcels or fragments, at least some of which are stored outside of conscious awareness. Then the body and the deep recesses of the unconscious psyche become repositories for the fragments of traumatic memory.

In the case of early developmental trauma, occurring in utero, or during birth, infancy or early childhood, the entire traumatic event and its impacts

> …the trauma response results in fragmentation and constriction, both of which are antithetical to the experience of spaciousness and joy.

typically are repressed, i.e., stored outside conscious awareness. When trauma occurs in adulthood, cognitive awareness of the traumatic event may not be entirely lost from awareness, but likely some of the affective and somatic components of trauma will be split off and preserved outside of consciousness. This divided state, while serving immediate survival, is not optimal in the long run.

Since trauma involves a fragmentation of experience, access to sustained joy becomes hampered, since joy is based upon unitive states of being. Ongoing access to joy can be restored following trauma—provided that the undischarged, constricted energy in the body is released and the parceled-out fragments of trauma memory are reclaimed in conscious awareness. Consequently, in the healing of trauma, images—which act as the integrative glue that binds together the experiential elements of cognition, affect and sensation—play a central role in recovering the memory and experience of trauma (Kalshed, 1997). Dreams—which are compositions of imagery, affect, sensation and cognition—possess an uncanny radar for locating unconscious sites where the unprocessed shards of traumatic memory are tucked away.

To recap, fragmentation of experience, somatic freezing and contraction are the chief defensive mechanisms activated in trauma. The response of somatic constriction is has been observed at the cellular level. If a single cell is prodded with a sharp instrument, the cell contracts and recedes. With the removal of the sharp point, the contraction releases, and the cell resumes its normal shape. However, if the prick is repeated several times, the cell retains its constriction, even upon withdrawal of the intruding instrument (Judyth O. Weaver, personal communication, April 4, 1995).[2] The microscopic response of the single cell highlights the fundamental organismic response to trauma: constriction. Contraction entails shifting into a state of increased compression and density. Thus, trauma generates *densities of existence*.

In human beings, the *densities of existence* that form following trauma are both physical and psychological. Bodily tissue, especially the tissue most directly affect by the traumatic assault, contracts, just as the single cell organism does. The body forms places of holding or even armoring in reaction to external threats. Similarly, in reaction to trauma, the human psyche contracts from its natural state of openness, trust, expansiveness, and participation. Expansiveness turns into contraction, trust into distrust, openness into defensiveness, participation into alienation.

If trauma is severe, contraction will

also be severe, such that these *densities of existence* can become the primary psychological landscape inhabited by a heavily traumatized person. When a contracted state becomes dominant within a person's psychology, such as when there is recurring trauma, it can be mistakenly regarded as the baseline or norm of existence. With recurring traumas and overlapping contractions within the body-psyche, a person can lose touch with the ability to imagine the possibilities of open, expansive, and participative states of being.

States of Contraction in Dreams

Expansive states—a living potential across the continuum of the cosmos—exist in dynamic interplay with contracted states, associated with danger and trauma. Given these twin realities, built into the deep structure of the cosmos and the deep structure of the human psyche, how then are expansive states and spacious awareness to be realized? How does one transform the trauma-based *densities of existence* into the expansive joy of participation?

In order to answer this question, in this section, I delve deeper into dream imagery depicting states of contraction, along with practices for metabolizing these chilling images. For in order to shift the frozenness of trauma into the spaciousness of bliss, images of constriction, appearing either during waking or dreaming, must be faced and engaged. Drawing on my personal story, I consider three dreams that depict the crushing weight of trauma upon the body-psyche.

To discover how expansive bliss can be wrested from the trials and travails of life has formed a lifelong personal quest, as my fate was forged in the crucible of trauma, when the birth canal was transfigured into a chamber of trauma and torture. My birth involved two simultaneous assaults, and my birth story was subsequently pieced together as young adult from the fragments of my birth story as told by my mother, images provided by my dreams, and the traces of somatic memory etched into my body.

Stanislav Grof's extensive research on birth trauma (1985) provides a theoretical framework for understanding birth trauma, and its profound impact on the psyche. Through techniques enabling deep unconscious exploration, Grof discovered the perinatal layer of the psyche, a bridge between the personal and collective unconscious. He identified four psychological stages of birth, concomitants of the biological stages of birth, deemed by him to be elemental perceptual structures underlying all of human experience.

In the first stage, or basic perinatal matrix (BPM I), the fetus floats unperturbed in the amniotic fluid in a state of oceanic bliss. This unitive state is mythologically associated with paradise and experiences of boundarylessness and cosmic spaciousness (Grof, 2012). However, disturbances to BPM I are often related to toxic changes in the body of the pregnant mother, typically experienced by the fetus as a dark and ominous threat and sense of being poisoned (Grof, 2012).

The second stage of birth, BPM II, is associated biologically with the constriction of uterine contractions when the cervix is not yet open, while psychologically, it is experienced a torturous, hellish confinement from which there is no-exit, arousing intense anxiety and existential despair (Grof, 2012). BPM III, the death-rebirth struggle, occurs after the cervix opens as the baby is propelled through the birth canal. Psychologically it entails a titanic struggle of extreme suffering, enduring strong pressures and intense energies, along with possible contact with biological material. BPM IV, the death-rebirth experience, is associated biologically with emergence from the birth canal the mother to initiate the birth process. The dose of Pitocin given instigated an unnatural, forced labor, with extreme contractions appearing from nowhere in rapid succession, violently pounding my head, catapulting me from the womb like a cannon ball. Meanwhile my mother was given a spinal block, making her unaware of the entire process.

Thus, I was flooded by toxicity while being violently beaten. These assaults became imprinted throughout my impressionable body-psyche. Adding insult to injury, I was born into an upwardly-ambitious family in the ego-driven, power-hungry D.C. area, for whom my suffering was invisible, with the expectation that I be normal and fit in, while adding my own achievements to the mix. The imposition of these social expectations meant excruciating social torment for my already-tattered soul.

As a young child, there were continuing assaults to my head, replaying what I endured in the tumultuous exit from the womb. My head became a strange

> ...in order to shift the frozenness of trauma into the spaciousness of bliss, images of constriction, appearing either during waking or dreaming, must be faced and engaged.

and severing of the umbilical cord, and psychologically with emergence into the light and liberation (Grof, 2012).

Birth Trauma: A Personal Story

As an RH factor baby, my blood type (O negative) and my mother's blood type (O positive) were fundamentally incompatible. In this situation, during labor the mother's body registers the baby as a foreign entity and seeks to combat it biochemically, producing a toxic situation for the baby. As a result, I was born jaundiced. Secondly, my birth was medically induced, albeit for no medical reason. For the sheer convenience of the doctor, the drug Pitocin was utilized in order to produce my birth one hour following the preceding birth. Pitocin, a synthetic drug, mimics the natural hormones of attractor for trauma, as if something initiated in the womb was destined to recur throughout my childhood. My existence took hold under a dark spell, with an uncanny series of assaults to my head occurring repeatedly.

As a toddler I found myself suspended at the throat between the crib bars, nearly suffocating, hanging on for dear life, leaving the imprint of an early near-death experience. Two permanent scars, seared into my brow and forehead, marked early childhood clashes against the hard edges of dense reality. Then at biking age, while riding serpentine patterns in the street, my head hit the pavement, resulting in a concussion. Late childhood years brought headaches, which intensified into torturous migraines in young adulthood.

This layering of traumas is related to Stanislav Grof's concept of COEXes, systems of condensed experience. "A COEX system consists of emotionally charged memories from different periods of our life that resemble each other in the quality of emotion or physical sensations that they share" (Grof, 2012, p. 38). Moreover, each COEX constellation, as a thematically-recurring experiential pattern, tends—

> to be superimposed and anchored in a particular aspect of the trauma of birth... [T]he experience of birth is so complex and rich in emotions and physical sensations that it contains the elementary themes of all conceivable COEX systems in a prototypical form... [T]he COEX systems [are] general organizing principles of the human psyche (Grof, 2012, p. 39).

Dreams of Contraction: Personal Examples

The crushing weight and devastating impact of these various head traumas coalesced in a dream in 2006:

> *It is nighttime in the city. I'm out partaking of city life. I return late in the night to find my car, left behind in a nearly-empty parking lot, infused with a cast of golden orange light from street lamps. Glancing across the lot, I spot my car, whose body has been entirely crushed. The crushed car body sits loosely on top of the chassis and wheels, which are completely intact. Stunned, in disbelief, my first thought forms: "Who can I call to get this damage repaired?" I fear no one will agree to repair it, as this kind of damage gets labeled "totaled" and is sent to the junk yard. Still, the name 'Car Care Center' comes to mind.*

This image of the crushed car body was shocking and disturbing, yet it brought almost no affect. For several days, I was completely numb, a resurfacing of the freezing response. However, I immediately recalled a related dream from two days prior, in which I was being relentlessly chased by a man driving a crushing machine (similar to the Zamboni machines used to resurface ice skating rinks). In a series of scenes, I am running from the crushing machine, attempting to escape the threat of being crushed to death. This dream elicited intense fear, and I awoke in an adrenaline-soaked state of hyper alert, as if running for my life.

The dream of the crushing machine called up a much earlier dream from about fifteen years prior, in the early 1990s, during young adulthood when I was first exploring dreams and uncovering early traumas:

> *I am driving my car into the Lincoln or Holland tunnel in New York City, in heavy traffic that spirals downward, becoming ever more tightly compressed as it descends into the dark abyss of the tunnel. As the tunnel walls narrow, vehicles move together into greater density and concentration, metal boxes on wheels closing in on me.. Pressing nearest to me are two 18-wheeler trucks, with cranes and booms swinging loosely overhead. An ominous fear of being crushed to death engulfs me like pall.*

The tunnel imagery also suggests my harrowing passage through the birth canal. My therapist and I felt this image depicted the near crushing of my ego as a young being, a near miss with psychosis. In the two more recent car dreams, at first, I run in fear, trying to escape the crushing machinery, while in the second dream, two days later, the dreaded outcome has occurred, the crushing forces have prevailed, the damage has been done to the car body. Fear is replaced by shock, disbelief, and numbness.

While seeking to digest this stark image, an analogy came to mind: the initiation of an Eskimo shaman who is taken out into the desolate cold for weeks or months, to contemplate his skeleton, while rubbing stones together. Being reduced to his skeleton, his initiation is completed when he receives the ritual name for each of his bones (O'Kane, 1994). The stark image of the crushed car body similarly symbolizes nearly complete destruction of the personality.

Cars in dreams often symbolize the body, as the body is the vehicle enabling movement through the world. After a day had passed, I was able to identify the portion of my physical body represented by the body of the crushed car, and also to notice that the chassis and tires beneath the car body were not crushed, but instead intact. It seemed that the chassis and tires referred to my hip structure and legs, the base and mobile parts, while the car body represents my upper body—torso and head—all that "sits" upon the base of hips and legs. The intact chassis and tires indicated that a portion of my body-psyche had not been crushed by the various traumas, but was still intact, allowing life to go on, without caving into a disintegration of the ego.

When bringing my attention to settle in the hip region, along the boundary between these two parts—the crushed car body and the intact chassis—I experienced a quickening of vitality. To my surprise, an abundance of trapped energy was collected here! Initially this appeared as a narrow yet steady stream of vitality flowing from beneath and beyond my familiar identity. Along this boundary, I contacted the presence of spaciousness, a flow of life force that both connected and grounded me. In contact with this bubbling of life energy, my sense of self became more relaxed, open, and spacious. Meditating on the chassis image, and becoming aware of the sensations pulsating along the hip line, I felt the old-compacted identity, built on top of the chassis, dissipating.

A shift from the crushing weight of trauma into spacious openness, vitality and joy was now transpiring. In order for the compressed density of trauma to be transformed into the exuberance of joy, the image of the crushed car body, and its associated affects and sensations, needed to be attended to, digested and integrated in conscious awareness.

Where trauma has been prominent, the road to joy travels through a psychosomatic landscape in which states of compression and contraction are prominent features, acting as monuments of memory to earlier atrocities. Dreams, together with the altered consciousness of the hypnopompia, impart a precious gift, providing lucid access to these intensified states of contraction, as well as images and memories of earlier crushing experiences. I discovered that giving respect, attention, and receptive awareness to bodily sites of contraction, along with the associated imagery, opens the way to release and joy.

The hypnopompic state offers the ideal moment to work with the altered consciousness of both expansion and

WINTER 2023   37

contraction. The energetic openings during hypnopompia are pure gifts from the dreaming realm, naturally bestowed by the sleep cycle without any effort on our part; in mythic terms, they are gifts from the god of sleep and dreams, Hypnos. When trauma has been buried and repressed, he hyper lucidity of hypnopompia is tantamount to a grace granted by the spirit realm, shining a light beam on the dynamics of expansion and contraction, thereby allowing a release of constriction and entry into spaciousness.

Transforming Contraction into Expansion

Given that our lives, like the universe itself, are set within the dynamic forces of contraction and expansion, how might the suffering of contraction transformed into the sublimity of expansion? Certainly, spaciousness must be cultivated amidst life's inevitable assaults together with the proneness of the body-psyche to constrict and develop densities in response to trauma. Joy must be set free within the spaces of the soul's suffering.

Amidst the trials and tribulations of life, there is embedded within the soul a relentless longing, perhaps even imperative, to realize the ecstasy of expansive states of being. Bliss arises with moments of opening, when contraction relaxes its tight survival grip into the spaciousness of being. Thus, there is a bodily basis, a somatic ground, that participates in the manifestation and sustenance of authentic joy. As joy is embodied and realized somatically (through releasing the densities of contraction held in the body), there is a potential that emerges, of cultivating spaciousness as an abiding way of being.

The interplay of expansion and contraction within the microcosm of the human being is derivative of macrocosmic dynamics of expansion and contraction. Contemporary physicists tell us that the universe both arises from and expresses elemental dynamics of contraction and expansion. The Big Bang, the explosive expansion into creation, emanates outward from an unfathomable density of compressed energy, the original black hole. Indeed, the world composed of multiple things, so majestically displayed before our eyes, emerges from a balanced tension between the forces of outward expansion and gravitational contraction that coheres matter and objects together.

The universe thrives on the edge of a knife. It if increased its strength of expansion it would blow up; if it decreased its strength of expansion it would collapse. By holding itself on the edge it enables a great beauty to unfold... By holding itself in the peace of a fecund balance of tensions, it enables planetary structures and living beings to blossom forth. Every being that thrives does so in a balance of creative tension (Swimme and Berry, 1992, p. 54).

Thus, consciously engaging states of contraction and expansion within the body-psyche deepens our conscious participation in the primordial patterns and organizing principles of the cosmos.

I adopt the primary framework of expansion and contraction based upon the imagery of the dreams discussed in this paper, as well as my direct experience of the fluctuations of the energy body in the hypnopompic state of consciousness. (While Peter Levine also incorporates certain metaphors from physics and chemistry into the trauma literature, he operates from a primarily contraction/expansion Newtonian model that does not incorporate advances in complexity theory—where concepts of fragmentation and reintegration have assumed greater importance.)

There is, however, a tendency for sites of contraction within the body-psyche to fall outside of awareness, to become hidden in shrouds of numbness, where the link between awareness and sensation is severed. Like black holes in space, these densities of the flesh become isolated from participation in the greater life force,

> *Observing sites of density with unflinching awareness creates a spacious environment for the knot of density to relax and release, yielding a quickening of energy.*

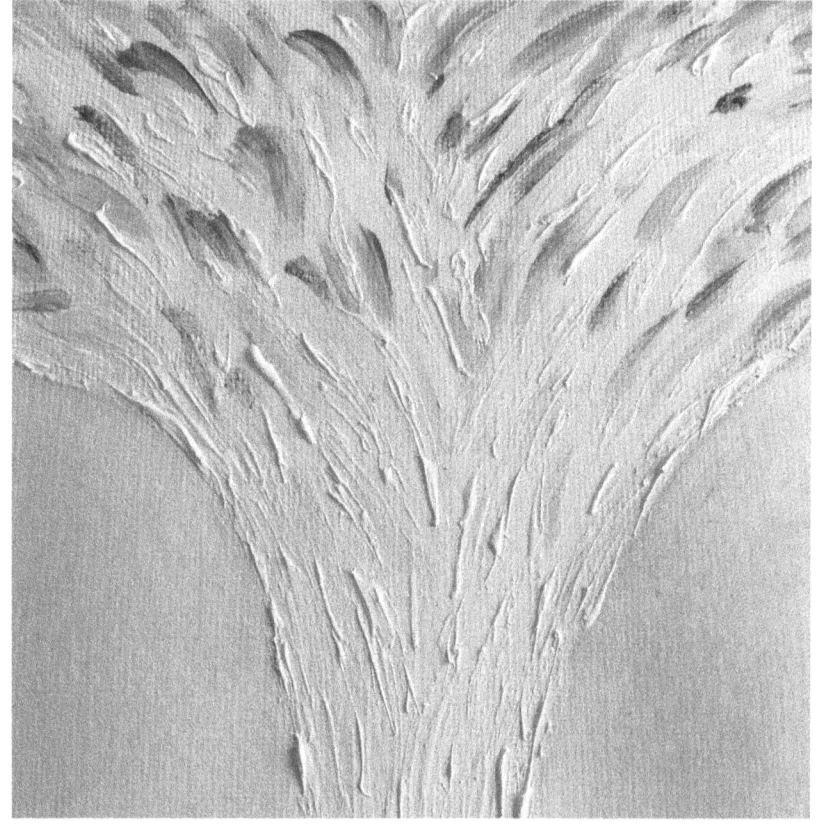

forming dark holes where the light of joy is banished. Human embeddedness in these harsh densities of the body can lead to a turning away from the universal life process. Caught in the contraction side of the polarity, one can become severed from natural participative states and joy.

What restores these *densities of existence* to the joy of participation in the greater whole? According to Aftab Omer, awareness serves as the primary "transmuting agent" (personal communication, August 3, 2006).[3] Conscious awareness must meet the sites of density within the body-psyche by using the muscle of attention. Attention directs psychic energy, thereby carrying power to shift these densities, melting frozen states of numbness. As awareness turns towards, rather than away from, these sites of density in the body-psyche, surrendering to the experience of tightening constriction, a surprising quickening of vitality and movement occurs.

Held within the sites of numbness and density in the body-psyche are earlier, perhaps forgotten, injuries that have receded from awareness and from life. Symptoms presenting as numbness and density are not meaningless, as they can superficially appear to be, but deeply meaningful traces relating directly to one's biographical storehouse of experiences. With the sustained presence of the observing self, the memory of a prior assault, which initially shows up in zones of numbness, c breaks through the barrier erected to keep awareness out. Freud describes with eloquence this pivotal shift in consciousness—from victim to self-empowerment—which entails embracing the trauma as a worthy opponent:

> [The patient] must find the courage to direct his attention to the phenomena of his illness. His illness must no longer seem contemptible, but must become an enemy worthy of his mettle, a piece of his personality, which has solid ground for existence, and out of which things of value for his future life have to be derived. The way is thus paved... for a reconciliation with the repressed material which is coming to expression in his symptoms, while at the same time a place is found for a certain tolerance for the state of being ill (Freud, 1914, p. 152).

Observing sites of density with unflinching awareness creates a spacious environment for the knot of density to relax and release, yielding a quickening of energy.

Theoretical Application

Cultivating expansive states paradoxically means attending to sites of contraction. Archetypal theory illuminates how the power of attention can transfigure contraction into expansion. Within archetypal theory, Jung theorized that archetypes partake of a bi-polar structure, organized according to positive and negative poles (Neumann, 1972). When an archetypal pattern intensifies and reaches its extremity of expression at either pole, there is a tendency for that pole to revert towards its opposite, similar to a pendulum that swings i in the other direction after reaching the far edge of its swing. Based on this principle, a shift towards the positive expansive pole can be affected in consciousness simply

Trauma, dreams, and hypnopompic experiences together offer sacred portals into the saturation of being.

by a willingness to consciously suffer the intensities of contraction. Thus, one way to catalyze a shift from contraction towards expansion is to bring sustained concentrated attention to bear upon the contracted pole.

These states of contraction, black holes of being, initially feel dark, foreboding and impenetrable. The light of consciousness tends to avoid and resist contact with such impenetrable density. However, if the initial resistance to approaching these black holes of being can be overcome, a transforming movement towards spaciousness can occur.

Bringing the light of consciousness to shine upon sites of contraction within the body-psyche first requires cultivating the discipline of mindfulness, with a steady, unswerving attention, followed by allowing the gaze of the observing self to focus and rest in communion with the impenetrable density. Gradually, with practice, consciousness develops muscle to meet the intensity of density with unswerving awareness. Using the muscle of attention, a back-and-forth movement can occur, between the spaciousness of awareness and the dense zones that hold the compressed energies of traumatic memory. Eventually a rapprochement takes place between the two, such that an interactive field constellates between spacious awareness and somatic density.

The observing self, making the offering of sustained attention, naturally is affected and altered by coming into the presence of these psycho-somatic black holes. Conscious contact with density has a slowing influence on consciousness—just as matter in a solid state moves at a slower vibration than matter in a gaseous state. In addition to this slowing, stilling effect, meeting the deposits of density within the body-psyche imparts a profoundly concentrated quality to consciousness. By holding the dense knots within a field of observing awareness, consciousness itself gains greater concentration and coherence, shifting toward a more unified state of organization. The flighty, scattering effects of dissociation are gradually gathered into greater singularity. Consequently, attending to density generates internal coherence. As traumatized consciousness gathers back the scattered fragments into itself, in turn it receives the gift of a more coherent and concentrated center. As resistance to approaching the densities in one's body-psyche fades, this concentrated centering of consciousness can become quite pleasant.

This dynamic interplay between spacious awareness and sites of somatic density, in which density gradually yields to and shifts into spaciousness, allows for a monumental figure-ground shift in perception and experience. This dance between density and spaciousness within consciousness has parallels at the material level of physical matter and empty space. While solid objects have conceded to the forces of gravitational contraction in order to come into existence, in fact they are composed of much more spaciousness than their appearance of solidity suggests to the naked eye. Thus, spaciousness underlies the outward appearance of density, both at the level of material objects and within consciousness.

Hence if engagement between awareness and density can be sustained, one mysteriously discovers its opposite—spaciousness—thereby unlocking the vitality and joy hidden within the apparent density. Bringing the spaciousness of awareness into communion with the densities of the body-psyche—that is, assimilating the numbness, heaviness, sadness, grief—the entire depressive downward turn of the soul associated with the residue of trauma—allows for a release of energy and an opening to joy.

Tolerating the sensations of density within the body tends to put one in touch with the deep well of grief held within the body. Grief, often experienced as dense sensation within the body, moves at a slow, almost still pace. It nearly stands still, and at times does. It silences. Surrendering into this still silence, detaching from all mental knowing and images, an ego death occurs. The traumatized identity ((in my dream, represented by the crushed body of the car), originally constructed to shut out awareness of trauma, dies. With this ego death, the stream of life stirs afresh with quickening movement (signified by chassis and wheels), partaking of greater spaciousness.

Conclusion

The vulnerable body that suffers the ordeal of trauma undergoes a contraction into the *densities of existence*. The frozenness of the traumatized body possesses a kinship with the stones, in whose density is hidden unimaginable energy, and vitality. The one who would know expansive joy as an abiding companion is paradoxical, asked to travel the continuum of the cosmos, befriending the densities of existence. This awake self who communes with contraction thereby transforms *densities of existence* into *concentrations of being*. While the densities of existence entail a closing off and retreat from life, this concentration of being is available for deepened participation in life and for expansive consciousness. For within the *concentration of being* is the dwelling place of the sacred, where joy abides and abounds. For the sacred is the saturation of being (Aftab Omer, personal communication, April 20, 2005).

Trauma, dreams, and hypnopompic experiences together offer sacred portals into the saturation of being. Dreams are symbol-rich—symbol in Greek literally means to throw together. With their multi-textured symbolism, activation of subtle body energies, and tendency to disturb the solidified structures of the egoic personality, dreams provide special access to the spaciousness of existence that is the essence of joy. Learning to pause and attend to the hypnopompic states that release the subtle energies of expansion and contraction accelerates the process of human growth at the depths of being.

While the "saturation of being" is offered initially as an evocative metaphor, phenomenologically it speaks to necessary, fate-driven encounters with experiences of density. As consciousness seeks to liberate itself from the constrictions of density, it vacillates, like a pendulum, between spacious awareness and contraction. These alternating states of expansion and contraction, and the symbolic imagery that accompanies them, feed and fuel the development of a soul that is saturated with being.

Thus, the traumatized individual, who undergoes trauma, enduring the tightening aperture of the freeze response, is invited to consciously know and intimately partake of the elemental dynamics of the universe, the dynamics of contraction and expansion. And this primal experience of participation confers a sense of belonging deeply, elementally, to the cosmos.

Footnotes

[1] While this article focuses on the role of dreams in releasing the freeze response of trauma, it should be noted that not all responses to life-threatening situations result in freezing and constriction. For some persons, traumatic threats are associated not with contraction but with an experience of greater lightness or diffusion in their sense of being. One example is the near-death experience, which may include some of the following elements, contributing not to contraction but to an experience of expansion: dissociation or detachment from the body, levitation with a view of one's body from above, transcendent peace and or bliss, security, warmth, surrender and dissolution, and the presence of light. However, whenever dissociation occurs, the psycho-spiritual-social task of integration afterwards still remains.

[2] Judyth O. Weaver is certified in Reichian Therapy, Somatic Experiencing, massage, Biodynamic Craniosacral Therapy, Pre- and Perinatal Therapy and teacher of Tai Chi Chuan, the Rosen Method and Sensory Awareness.

[3] Aftab Omer's work focuses on the emergence of human capacities within transformative learning communities and assisting organizations in tapping the creative potentials of conflict, diversity, and complexity.

References

Boznak, R. (2007). *Embodiment: Creative imagination in medicine, art and travel*. Abingdon-on-Thames, UK: Routledge. doi:10.4324/9780203961391

Campbell, J. (1988). *The power of myth*. New York, NY: Doubleday. doi:

Damasio, A. (1999.) *The feeling of what happens: Body and emotion in the making of consciousness*. New York, NY: Harcourt Brace. doi:10.26439/persona2000.n003.1708

Freud, S. (1914). Remembering, repeating and working-through (Further recommendations on the technique of psycho-analysis II). *The standard edition of the complete psychological works of Sigmund Freud, Volume XII (1911-1913): The case of Schreber, Papers on technique and other works*, 145-156. doi:10.1037/e417472005-288

Freud, S. (1953). *The interpretation of dreams*. New York, NY: Random House. doi:10.1037/e417472005-107

Gendlin, E. (1981). *Focusing*. New York: Bantam. doi:

Gendlin, E. (1986). *Let your body interpret your dreams*. Wilmette, IL: Chiron Publications. doi:

Grof, S. (1985). *Beyond the brain: Birth, death and transcendence in psychotherapy*. Albany, NY: SUNY Press. doi:

Grof, S. (2012). *Healing our deepest wound: The holotropic paradigm shift*. Newcastle, WA: Stream of Experience Productions. doi:

Hobson, J. A. (2002). *Dreaming: An introduction to the science of sleep*. Oxford University Press. doi: 10.1093/actrade/9780192802156.003.0001

Jaenke, K. A. (2004). Ode to the Intelligence of Dreams. *ReVision: Journal of Consciousness and Transformation.*, Vol. 27, No. 1, 2-8. doi: 10.3200/revn.27.1.2-48

Jung, C. G. (1960). *The structure and dynamics of the psyche. Collected Works, Vol. 8*. London: Routledge and Kegan Paul. doi:10.1515/9781400850952

Kalsched, D. (1996). *The inner world of trauma: Archetypal defenses of the personal spirit*. London: Routledge. doi:10.1525/jung.1.2000.19.2.51

Levine, P. (1997). *Waking the tiger, healing trauma: The innate capacity to transform overwhelming experiences*. Berkeley, CA: North Atlantic Books. doi:

Mindell, A. (2002). *Working with the dreaming body*. Portland, OR: Lao Tse Press. doi:

Neumann, E. (1972). *The great mother: An analysis of the archetype*. Princeton, NJ: Princeton University Press. doi: 10.1515/9781400866106

O'Kane, F. (1994). *Sacred chaos: Reflections on God's shadow and the dark self*. Toronto: Inner City Books. doi: 10.1177/000842989602500127

Solms, M. (2000). Dreaming and REM sleep are controlled by different brain mechanisms. *Behavorial. Brain Science*, 23: 843-50. doi: 10.1017/s0140525x00003988

Swimme, B. and Berry, T. (1992). *The universe story*. San Francisco: HarperSanFrancisco. doi:

Van der Kolk, B. (2006). Clinical implications of neuroscience research in PTSD. *Annals of the New York Academy of Sciences*, p. 1-17. doi: 10.1196/annals.1364.022

Heart-Knowing, Somatic Dreaming, and Trans-subjectivity:

A Scholarly Personal Narrative

Daniel Deslauriers, PhD

On an early spring morning, I awaken with a simple but very touching dream. Dwight Hawai (a good friend of mine) and I are giving each other a hug. In the dream, we are exchanging a deep connection. In heartful embrace, both our chests connect. I feel a subtle quasi-electrical current is being exchanged heart-to-heart. With this, the dream ends.

Upon awakening, this special sensation in my chest continued. I became puzzled by the dream. This hypnopompic experience sparked me to ask seemingly simple questions, slowly opening multiple horizons of inquiry: How should I understand the connection that I felt so deeply in the dream? What, or who was it about? Why was Dwight the agent, and trigger, of this felt sense of fullness and love?

Focusing on the nature of the dream's relational experience, numerous aspects of dream relationality unfold. What arises in the meaning-making process depends on the questions we ask. For instance: could the dream be about what Dwight represents for me —a particular imago? Alternatively, is it about Dwight?—my concern for him. Could the dream be about Dwight and me—our friendship? Or was it about "being in one's heart"?

Each question foregrounds a particular aspect of the relationship that puts either "me" at the center of the inquiry, or "him" (Dwight), or "us" (i.e., our relationship) or "that" (i.e., 'being in one's heart").

One of the most striking aspects of this dream is how it offered a significant somatic bloom. Impactful dreams have a particular sensory and somatic character (Kuiken et al., 2006; Jaenke, 2000). The felt sense during the dream seemed to delight not only the dreambody (the subtle dream self, or dream ego), but extended to my physical body. Writing about the

---

Daniel Deslauriers, PhD is Professor in the Transformative Studies Doctorate at the California Institute of Integral Studies (CIIS) in San Francisco, and former chair of East-West Psychology program. Teacher, author and performer, he directs narrative, theoretical, and art-based research at CIIS. He co-wrote *Integral dreaming. A holistic approach to dreams* (Sage). His work intersects contemplative, transpersonal, and consciousness studies, as well as embodied relational practices, which led him to study and teach Contact Improvisation.

Photos: Daniel Deslauriers

hypnopompic experience, Daly (2016) asserts that the dream-waking state, or hypnopompia, is a unique liminal state through which the subtle body can be felt and through which "embodied knowledge and healing may be received and experienced" (p. iv). My dream confirms this: a unique somatic felt sense constellated around the heart, triggering a feeling that was still pulsing in me as I woke up. This lingering feeling, bridging both sleeping and waking, not only made the dream impactful and memorable but also was the spark of a further deepening embodied inquiry.

I offer this personal analysis of my dream in the spirit of Scholarly Personal Narrative (SPN) (Nash & Viray, 2014). This builds on the notions that stories are a complex mode of knowing (Deslauriers, 1992) and that personal narratives can enhance scholarly inquiry. I paid close attention to the unfolding details of my experience while engaging in an in-dwelling process that ties my felt-sense to intellectual inquiry. In other words, I followed the existential and philosophical questions that were opening in my attempt of meaning-making, while at the same time drawing far and wide from personal history, philosophical literature, and research.

I had the dream just as I was preparing for a conference on the topic of intersubjectivity in dreams. The dream became 'exhibit A' for that talk: my ideas were developed as I was tracing the complex lacing pattern between theory and experience. The meaning of the dream gradually unfolded as I was writing about it, sharing it with friends and family, and meticulously trying to answer the queries brought by those with whom I was sharing it.

Beginning with the central dream

image—the heartful embrace—I felt that it was pointing to the core nature of intersubjectivity, that is, the lived experience of a shared feeling. This sense of sharing may appear obvious at first glance and should not come as a surprise. That is, until we start peeling away the layers of our assumptions around the act of knowing, to discover that the very notion of "shared feeling" is not a given, echoing a theme that runs deeply into the very fracture of our modes of knowing, especially the ascendency of objectivity that privileges distance and detachment. In which way is the act of knowing connected to the place of 'knowing with'? Already here, is a clue to the relational nature of heart-knowing.

What is certain is that I do have a real friendship with Dwight in waking life, and the dream seemed to be sourcing from it. I had never dreamt of a male friend in this way. Our friendship had deepened when a few weeks before the dream, I offered to take him to the Hilo (Hawaii) hospital for his initial appointment for radiation and chemotherapy. I remember how deeply moved he was that I had offered to help. He told me that asking for help was not easy for him: for most of his life, he had been the one in the helping role. Now, the tables had turned, and he had to tame the feeling of awkwardness about receiving help. On the way to the appointment, our sharing brought both of us close to tears––a spontaneous emergence—where together we recognized how the acts of giving and receiving are core during times of shared vulnerability. With life and death providing an existential backdrop, the somatic felt sense of the preciousness of friendship was only sharpened; there was no time for pretense.

Called by my teaching tasks on the continent, I had to leave Hawaii. I did not see him for the entirety of his treatment, which was completed when I had the dream.

So, the dream came as a surprise. I had booked a flight back to Hawaii the day before the dream and perhaps the dream was in anticipation of my return. However, that return was not to be, opening a new relational twist heralded by the dream.

Two days after the dream, I received a call from my brother in Montreal alerting me that my father was now lying in the hospital, nursing a heart problem, something that, at 91, he had never suffered before. When I asked my brother when my father was taken to the hospital, he told me the Thursday prior—the very morning I had the dream. The phone call immediately brought back the dream and thrust upon it a new light. The connection with the heart took on an almost literal significance. At that moment, the dream took on a telepathic bent. I saw the dream as foreshadowing that something is the matter with the heart. It was compelling me to put my attention on the life of the heart.

The dream, with its straightforward intersubjective theme, was beginning to shape my response to this unwelcome news about my father. While the dream started with Dwight, it was now giving me hints on how to be with my father, in this new situation. Now I perceived it as a call to get closer to my father, as the dream image of the hug emphasized proximity. More meaningfully though, it was an invitation to take action "from the heart."

With this recognition about acting from the heart, the dream inquiry further deepened [1].

Indeed, by then the dream was starting to fuel an inquiry into the nature of heart knowing. What does it mean to act "from the heart"? How should I understand this dream admonition for closer proximity? As empathy? Compassion? Respect? As engaging from a loving place? As a special way to be present, to listen, and to "co-feel" with a parent? In the context of elder care, these questions took on a particular trajectory. What does it mean to enter the place of the heart with an elder parent whose perception of the world is becoming increasingly disconnected from consensual reality because of dementia, whereby the very texture of intersubjectivity is fraying?

Intersubjective and Transsubjective Awakening—a Theoretical Interlude

The intersubjective view of dreaming pushes back against the commonsense notion that dreams are mainly a personal display of images and sensations. The fact that dreams arise autonomously in sleep when we disconnect from those around us and unplug from our electronic devices, heightens the perception of subjective isolation. Dreams may be uniquely and subjectively "ours," intimating a deeper connection to self. Still, they do not belong exclusively to the subjective realm. For even if we are the sole creator and experiencer of our dreaming, the "Other" does not vanish.

On the contrary, most of our dreams contain people with whom we interact and share the dream space. Researchers have proposed that the purpose of dreaming may be to track the constant changes in the complex relational web within waking life (Kahn and Hobson, 2005; McNamara, 2004).

We dream so that we can figure out pathways of meaning and action within the many intersubjective spaces we inhabit. For example, authors have shown how

> *What does it mean to act "from the heart"? A special way to be present, to listen, and to "co-feel" with a parent?*

dreams are making personal commentary on social events linked to our relational world (Lippman, 1998; Meltzer, 2009). Others have shown how the dream is polyphonic in nature, as an amalgam of the voices of the self and others. This begs the question: What are the limits of intrapsychic space when it is 'overflowing' in many ways, since the dreamer is part of an 'intersubjective chain' (Kaës, 2002, p. 77)?

Dream imagery is often interlaced with emotions and affect that at once disclose, color and structure the nature of the many relationships we inhabit at any given time (Demos, 1995; Tomkins, 1982). Simply put, dreaming helps us to metabolize the relational ins and outs of our social waking life (Bogzaran and Deslauriers, 2012).

What these authors and researchers' findings share in common is the relational dynamics that form the basis of the dreaming experience. Furthermore, Hall (1972) and Domhoff (1996) have shown that the waking-dreaming continuity is scaffolded around personal relationships earlier captured in the research of Hall and Van de Castle (1966).

Of course, not all cultures make a sharp dichotomy between waking and dreaming experiences as is typical in the West (Tedlock, 2005), nor is the nature of the self fully distinct from that of the group or the ecological matrix (Colorado, 2021, Kimmerer, 2021).

Drawing from evolutionary theory, the work of Revonsuo and Valli (2000) proposes a "threat simulation theory" of dreaming, including those posed by others. While this theory helps make sense of the place of vigilance about (social) threats, it falls short of explaining the more positive and altruistic dreams such as the Heartful Embrace dream. We do not just rehearse threat scenarios in dreams, but also virtuous or beneficial scenarios as well. To rehearse such scenarios may be just as essential in facing complex social events, such as the long-term care of infants, or of a parent at the end of life.

To reflect this, Revonsuo, Tuominen and Valli (2015) more recently proposed a Social Simulation Theory of dreaming, whereby dreams immerse us into a virtual social reality as a means to practice "evolutionary important functions of social perception and social bounding" (p 23).

A new branch of brain research known as social neuroscience seeks to understand the foundational role of relationality in human life (Todorov, Fiske & Prentice, 2011), and within which the central role of dream relationality, including the orienting role of dream affect, fits very well. In particular, some have sought to better understand prosocial behavior and altruism (Pfaff, 2015), which address virtuous emotions such as found in the Heartful Embrace dream.

For his part, Breton (2008) hypothesized a social mapping function for dreaming: "the neurophysiology of dreaming may have been a preadaptation for the evolution of hominid consciousness" by locating the dreamer "in emotionally salient social space, a trait possibly derived from hippocampal spatial mapping" (p. 379).

While the intersubjective nature of dreaming is becoming well established, the role of intersubjectivity in dream meaning making has not always followed suit. Since the latter quarter of the 20th century, dreamers have been cast as the primary arbiters of dream meaning. This is a core heuristic in dreamwork. However, this subjective focus should not become unduly narrow. To moor the dreaming mind on the shores of the self can shortchange the complexity of relational reality and that of our interdependence.

It is possible that subjectivity be skewed towards narcissism—that is, a limited view of subjectivity fed by a cultural narrative positioning the interior self against the social, cultural, and ecological matrices within which we are embedded. Surely, focusing on the private and individual nature of dreaming is important, yet it is possible to overlook the many ways in which dreaming draws from our relational and communal life.

Fortunately, in therapeutic settings, dream meaning-making is best understood as a collaborative practice between client and therapist (Bonime, 1989; Hill, 2003), a collaboration that may help re-center the relational dimension of dreaming, with the knowledge that dreaming can affect and inform the many relationships and "we-spaces" we inhabit (Deslauriers, 2011).

Anthropologist Tim Ingold (2014) speaks of the etymology of the words "subjective" and "objective," sharing in common the Latin root, jacere, which means to throw. This ties to the phenomenological insight that we are always already there, "thrown" into the world, improvising on the stage of life. A softer and less projectile version of this could be delineated as follows: intersubjectivity is about finding our way in the field of knowledge that is already there in the co-emergence "between" and "amongst" people. For instance, I only know the nature of shared feeling—such as it was pointed out to me in the dream, as a quality of being in one's heart—by experiencing this feeling with another (even if I might never know if the feelings shared are precisely the same).

In line with psychoanalyst Bracha Ettinger (2006), beyond relational intersubjectivity lies a more primal "matrixial"— trans-subjectivity. The world itself acts as a larger container of experience. This refers to a womb-like space that is not just subjective, nor merely intersubjective.

Rather, the pregnant matrix that contains all subjects provides the space within which all experience always already takes place. In this way, the matrixial nature of the world is transsubjective. trans-subjectivity is defined (by Merriam-Webster) as 'relating to, or being in a state of existence independent of an individual mind or mode of thinking though not necessarily independent of the modes of thought common to all [people].' I take this to mean that dimensions of life and experience have an objective reality independent of me, but that it takes me (or a subjective mind) to perceive them.

I propose here the radical concept of **reciprocal embeddedness** to unfold this further. The subjective mind acts as a womb: it "holds" and co-creates our

> We dream so that we can figure out pathways of meaning and action within the many intersubjective spaces we inhabit.

world. At the same time, we are simultaneously held by the world within which we are a tiny part and are continuously reborn into through the life-process of becoming and participation. While intersubjectivity speaks to the dance that takes place between people, trans-subjectivity points to the participatory dance between two matrices: the mind—my mind—that holds the world and the world that holds my being and my mind.

The dream of the Heartful Embrace points to a (re)awakening to the relational nature of experience. This awakening may propel us to act accordingly. The dream's theme, the co-embrace and its felt-sense, partakes of relational knowledge. From a knowing perspective, the dream discloses what having an "open heart" feels like. Importantly, the dream discloses this perspective phenomenologically.

In writing this article, I try to grasp and analyze this with my mind, to cognize it. Yet in the dream, a more direct knowledge is encapsulated within the experience itself. Just as we can awaken to the intersubjective core of our subjective life, we can also awaken to the matrixial dimensionality of interdependence.

Stated otherwise, if I remain closed from within my intrasubjective self-sense, I may never allow the matrixial world to reveal itself to me. On the other hand, that awakening can translate into a feeling and an open-ended knowing that I am being shaped by the world. I experience insight as myself 'growing' inside the world.

Yet all the while, my actions are reciprocally giving shape to the world. So matrixial awareness is an awareness of being part of a co-emergent process. To reiterate, the matrixial backdrop of intersubjectivity is 'transsubjective'. Something that exists beyond me and us, but that takes me –or us- to conceive of it.

As I try to distinguish and connect the notions of intersubjectivity[2] and trans-subjectivity, suffice here to say that the notion of trans-subjectivity points towards the fact that some form of incipient patterning gives shape to experience (Adams 2004, Conforti, 2003). Incipient patterning beckons us to the fact that many abstract notions, such as that of 'fairness' for example, can nevertheless organize our behavior, and social perception, despite the difficulty of ascribing an ontological basis to them, other than in rational or instinctual terms.

This orientation towards the organizing principle at play in the dream lead me to ask: Could it be that my dream came to me so that I could get in touch with, not just my relationship with Dwight or my father, but also heart knowing more generally? Although it may seem objectifying at first, such question opens us to look more closely at the "that" of the dream. Heart knowing, once identified, could be seen as a structuring dimension, or quality, that uniquely informs my relationships to Dwight, and my father, each in its own way. And by extension, I can interrogate its presence (or absence) in other relationships.

A Story Folding, Unfolding, and Refolding

The rich emotions that texture relationships are the fertile ground from which dreams grow, and where they cycle back

(Deslauriers, 2011). As psychoanalyst Paul Lippman (1998) writes, dreaming is the private voice that comments on our relational concerns. I propose that dreams do more than "comment" on our relational concerns. Dreams are occasions of experience. Beholding this fact, the enactive dimension of a dream comes into play in a radical way. In the simplest of terms, the enactive theory of dreaming can be couched as such: dreams give us the experience of "what it is like."

My dream with Dwight was not solely a comment on our connection; it was an actual enactment of what a heart-to-heart relationship can be. Within the perspective of knowledge as enaction, knowing is closely tied to the felt sense of the dream. And this is also why the somatic felt sense is such an important marker. The somatic bloom of the dream already embodies or inscribes into the experience a particular feeling tone: the quasi-electrical sensation. Further in time, in waking, the dream may help attune my actions, my thinking process, and my propensity to see the world in a particular way. In this case, it is about how to be more truthful to the open-heart dimension that the dream is disclosing.

From this perspective, the dream is not only about me (as primary subject), or about Dwight (as my relational counterpart, since I already know that Dwight is a warm-hearted person). The dream is also about the inherent dimension present in connection, such as that of the open-heartedness disclosed inside the felt sense. This knowing is not entirely new to me (at least at a conceptual level), yet the dream begs me to flesh out and expand the nature of this knowing.

As my inquiry deepened, the Heart-

ful Embrace dream started to provide a somatically felt compass that enabled me to discern how to engage with my father, whose prognosis only points towards a worsening decline.

Complementary to the notion of matrixial trans-subjectivity, Ettinger (2014) further points to the notion of primary compassion, which is a source of aesthetical and ethical openings where the fragility of the self meets the vulnerability of the others. As I meet the dream as an inquiry, the knowledge provided by the dream is both incipient and emergent. The beauty of the dream is that it makes me a participant and not just an observer.

In trying to find an answer as to why Dwight came into the dream as opposed to any other of my friends, I had to reach back further in my relationship with Dwight, touching on the nature of the therapeutic exchange. Dwight is a somatic practitioner in Hawaii where there exist many experimental treatments that push the usual boundaries of somatic practices. The actual space of Dwight's practice is a medium-sized and shoulder-deep pool warmed to body temperature.

There, through guided fluid movements initiated by him, he invites clients to silently enter a dream-like journey, which unfolds during the therapeutic hour, as he manipulates their body on the surface, as well as under the water. One could consider this 'only' a form of bodywork, as most of the hour-long session unfolds in silence. However, I attest that deep inner movement is taking place inside the space of this silent engagement since I received a treatment from Dwight about two years before the dream.

At the end of the treatment, he put me into a fetal position under the water, and held me there for the longest time, as long as my breath could effortlessly hold. Then as he gently pulled me out of the water, he held me in a full body embrace, with my head on his shoulder, the holding position we shared in the dream. And right at that moment, a flood of memories of my father holding me in his arms as a kid came rushing through.

There it is! I had found the answer I was looking for. A deep entanglement of somatic memories, folding back and forth in time, heart-to-heart with my father and me, as it was in my childhood, and with Dwight in the middle, as the midwife of this daydream. The water therapy had the effect of smoothing the edge of years of relational conflicts and opening new relational possibilities into present time.

This deep somatic felt sense came back to me all the way from childhood, inside a transference dream, if we consider that Dwight, in the dream, and in his practice, held a space for my father (in psychological transference, feelings, and expectations towards a parental figure are redirected towards the therapist).

Past and present interlace inside the somatic feeling of the dream. All the while, the incipient future is pointing forward. Just as it did between Dwight and me earlier, the table has turned between my father and me, as I become one of the caretakers for the body of my senior father. Now it is I who am holding him, while he was wading inside his own delirious dream.

I had found the source of the dream image in that water-enhanced therapeutic encounter, the very place my own relationship with my father was somatically unlocked and positively re-calibrated. And now, I see why it was important for that work to be done—so that I could show up for my father with something other than a bruised heart.

The day I arrived in Montreal, my father was just coming back from surgery. Fortunately, this surgery only entailed local anesthesia for inserting a pacemaker that would keep his weak heart beating. My father seemed to recognize me when I arrived, at least, that's what I gathered by the smile with which he greeted me. I did not test him by asking him to say my name.

After a week of daily visits, my brother finally asked him if he recognized me, and my father answered that I was a "good

friend." Eventually, with some prompting, he was able to say my name, looking down at the floor, as if he was sorry that he couldn't do it without help. At that moment, I knew that the usual intersubjective bonds of father-son were not playing out the same way for him. All week, I was his "good friend." And it was with sadness in my heart that I reconciled that I was not doing this for his recognition. The dream reminded me of the altruistic dimension of an open heart. Virtues usually associated with heart intelligence (Whitney, 2017) such as empathy, compassion, and care, are at their core other-centered.

The hospital environment that was, for me, in the past, almost repulsive, became a much more neutral and beneficial place, and I was not so anxious to leave. Acting from the heart seems to make tasks easier to be carried forth. It was allowing me to be more patient with him, however often he would ask the same question in short succession. That meant giving the same answer sometimes over 30 times in an hour. A narrowing of the relational space because of dementia meant I had to creatively find paths towards meaningful conversation, and towards his own heart space, reaching for his emotions and what he relished.

Although a simple dream, yet because it addresses a quality that is at the core of intersubjectivity, it opened up many layers of feeling and understanding. Addressing the subtle energy felt in the dream, my inquiry points out to its role in terms of the loving felt-sense that come with heart-knowing (see also Esser, 2013 for a discussion of subtle energy in spiritual dreams). The felt-knowing in my dream, centered in the heart, began to serve as a compass for right action, and provided the basis for beholding my own experience in a self-compassionate manner.

Cycling Back: Dream Sharing and Self-renewal

Viewed in the context of trans-subjectivity, incipient knowing is something that is always already present. The dream points to a shift toward heartful embrace, yet even if this shift is told as a personal story, it is not just something subjective. Heart knowing is possible for anyone who wishes to unfold the meaning of the heart in their own life. When we share dreams—itself a meaningful intersubjective enactment, as I am doing here with my own story—we may find that we enter a unique process of self-renewal.

Of course, this begs the question about what is being renewed. Perhaps, notions that we consider as understood become fresh again at a deeper level; what seems obvious—such as the subtle nature of shared feelings—opens up to a new inquiry. From this perspective, self-renewal has to do with aligning with what is true for oneself.

Years of observation of dream sharing in groups has shown me that the process of renewal doesn't stop with the self: others can feel renewed by hearing or resonating with someone else's dream and story. Perhaps the core of enacted sociality, the living culture into which we partake, may also be renewed by dreams and dream-sharing. Shulman and Strumsa (1999) wrote:

To tell one's dream... is always an overdetermined act or statement, at once situating the self in relation to a rich universe of cultural meanings and implied metaphysical intuitions and creating, or re-creating, that same universe from within (p. 3).

Here I deepen the theoretical points about the nature of intersubjectivity and trans-subjectivity as unfolded in dreams. Intersubjectivity is what is created and enacted when one's "interior" self encounters another's. In this meeting, a relational field is formed, shifting and moving according to the combined actions taken by those who participate in it. Through our habits of relating, we partake in the creation of interpersonal space, and at the same time, we receive the influence of others. Intersubjectivity is a pregnant field of potentiality, where meaning, with various degrees of mutuality, can be created, transmitted, constructed, exchanged, or sometimes imposed, twisted, or violated, or can even be hidden (as in family secrets) or denied (as when we withhold news from

others that we know would impact them) (Deslauriers, 2011).

All that we do with or onto others shapes the intersubjective field. Judith Blackstone (2007) writes: "In its simplest terms [. . .] intersubjectivity theory proposed [. . .] a transition from focus on the empowerment and fulfillment of the individual to an understanding of the individual as always in some sense in relationship with his or her own environment" (pp. 19-20).

The intersubjective field is dynamic and fluid as we constantly improvise our way forward in life. Since engaging in an intersubjective somatic practice called Contact Improvisation[3], I have become a keen observer of how dance is structured or scaffolded from the physics of our bodies. When we enter a "we" space, a group, or a relational dance, we are not just entering a blank space. As noted earlier, etymologically speaking, the "–ject" aspect of the word intersubjective, has us thrown into something that is already there for us. For example, we can generally speak of the "we-ness" of life by looking at what gives texture to our sociality, such as the linguistic code that allows our "common sense," our *sensis communis*, to circulate.

Alternatively, we could point to our transportation system; the monetary system that allows us to pay our dues or collect our salaries; the ways our food arrives at our table—all the institutions in which we partake, the we-spaces we journey in and out of. Woven through these social spaces are structuring patterns that shape the field, and which are value laden. Within the intersubjective field, the culture that we understand as ours holds in place particular patterns of relating that shape what we recognize as familiar. These are not to be re-invented each time; neither are they inconsequential.

Conclusion

This inquiry unfolded the renewing potential of a hypnopompic dream motif, providing a window to the nature of heart-knowing, and guiding me on how to be with my father at a delicate stage of his life.

The topography of my relationship with my father transformed during a therapeutic encounter where somatic relational memories were unlocked and reframed. Triggered by the Heartful Embrace dream, memories resurfaced after many years, as if on cue, leading me to explore how heart knowing can be enacted when called to be a caretaker. This shows how intersubjectivity is crucial in dream meaning-making, especially within a parent-son relationship, whose arc spans many decades.

This inquiry also explored the notion of trans-subjectivity and how it points to a preexistent and incipient knowing field (in this case, about heart knowing), yet one that gets disclosed through the enactment of it. The inquiry does not come to rest, but instead opens a broader ontological question about the enactment of heart knowing: What happens when intersubjective values and practices are seen not only as being co-created between people but also profoundly resonated with?

Ethical questions arise: how is life transformed when we let incipient values such as empathy and care co-structure our relational experiences? A stance that recognizes the existence of transsubjective reality can act as an existential counterpoint to an individual's creative agency: what comes into play is an open, listening mode of being that helps us recognize (and perhaps even surrender to) what is already there, ready-at-hand, ready-at-mind, or ready-at-heart inside relationships.

These structuring patterns provide the frame for incipient knowledge to inform our lives. It becomes possible (or more likely) to enact qualities of being that exist beyond our subjective experience, even as they are constitutive of our intersubjective relationships.

Such notions may be those of morality, compassion, forgiveness, intimacy, love. Or they could be those of diversity, inclusion, and social justice, etc. Such notions predate us; they have been the subject of moral teachings, and spiritual transmission for eons. Yet they are fresh for us to live anew. These notions don't seem to "grow stale" when we are called to enact them. My experience has shown me that

> *Trans-subjectivity points to the participatory dance between two matrices: the mind—my mind—that holds the world and the world that holds my being and my mind.*

with age, we can refine our perception of them as we inquire into them, taking them under the magnifying glass of a phenomenological gaze.

This includes imaginal experience encountered in dreams. Dreams like the Heartful Embrace can become emblems, a form of positive rehearsal for how to respond to broader societal issues, whereby those can be perceived through the prism of the heart.

In concluding, I take the liberty to expand the canvas of my inquiry, as a way to intimate how the knowledge of the heart connects us to the broader trans-subjective reality that is continuously infusing our day-to-day life. Relationships have a dreamlike quality. Like dreams, they are creative and open-ended.

One of the most critical challenges at this time is for us to learn to live together in a world when interpersonal differences brought about by diversity seem to explode the comfort of cultural uniformity and conformity, leading to countless shapes of self-identity and hybridity. Relational consciousness is the real frontier of more inclusive cultures (local or global), especially when we begin to take seriously the matrixial dimension described here. This implies the mutual recognition of our deep interdependence inside layered matrices of relating, where biography and biosphere unfold in mutuality, informed by cultures we partake of. Individual actions and awakenings, in turn, can impact the cultural matrixes and the biological (ecological) matrix of our shared world.

Paying attention to the intersubjective dimension of our dreams can help us form (and in-form) our relational skills. The Heartful Embrace dream is pointing to the transsubjective realities that lie beyond the entrapments of self-gratification so prevalent in market economies, or the comforts arising from religious (or quasi-religious) certitude.

Such dreams point to places where we can truly meet, as embodied complex beings, even when at different stages in our life process, such as that between father and son. Feminist author Susan Griffin (1996), succinctly states a hopeful outcome of this coming together between the inner and outer: "If human consciousness can be rejoined not only with the human body but with the body of the earth, what seems incipient in the reunion is the recovery of meaning within existence that will infuse every kind of meeting between self and the universe, even in the most daily acts, with an eros, a palpable love, that is also sacred" (p. 9).

Drawn on the broader canvas of our shared world, could it be that the Heartful Embrace dream intimates what this feels like?

Endnotes

1 This inquiry could find meaningful expansion in the rich material about the heart (e.g., the sacred heart or the spiritual heart) found in most religious traditions. An excellent transcultural exposé on heart intelligence, engaging various spiritual traditions, is found in Whitney (2017). In this paper however, I chose to keep my focus on an organic, phenomenological unfolding of the question, staying close to my experience and where that lead me.
2 Ettinger is not alone speaking about the transsubjective. Hillman (1983) speaks of a transsubjective dimension of the imagination, and a similar distinction can be found in Jung between the personal unconscious and the collective unconscious. In researching the word transsubjective, I found out that Jung did use the word (Jung, CW 7, p.98) to describe that aspect of the unconscious later qualified by his English-speaking followers as the 'objective psyche' (see Fordham, 1951 and Hall, 1983).
3 Contact Improvisation is a form of partnered dance, often practiced in silence, demonstrating how relating bodies meet and move in space, affording endless pathways of movement, lifts, rolls, inversion, compression, counterbalance, and so on, often at the edge of falling. This form of dance assumes a high degree of interpersonal somatic attunement and can become a significant source of insights about the nature of relationships, including the nature of communication, trust, commitment, shared/divergent goals, how to negotiate differences and various levels of skills, and revealing the potentials of interactive creativity (Novack, 1990; Stark-Smith, 2003).

References

Boznak, R. (2007). *Embodiment: Creative imagination*, Blackstone, J. (2007). *The empathic ground: Intersubjectivity and nonduality in the psychotherapeutic process*. Albany, NY: State University of New York Press

Bogzaran, F., & Deslauriers, D. (2012). *Integral Dreaming: A holistic approach to dreams*. Albany, NY: State University of New York Press.

Adams, V. M. (2008). *The archetypal school*. In Polly Young-Eisendrath & Terence Dawson (Eds), The Cambridge Companion to Jung (2nd Edition), 107-124. NY: Cambridge University Press.

Bonime, W. (1986). *Collaborative dream interpretation*. Journal of the American Academy of Psychoanalysis, 14 (1), 15-26.

Breton, D. P. (2008). *Dreaming, adaptation, and consciousness. The social mapping hypothesis*. Ethos, 28 (3). 379-409. doi.org/10.1525/eth.2000.28.3.379

Conforti, M. (2003). *Field, form, and fate: Patterns in mind, nature, and psyche*. Spring Publications.

Colorado, A. (2021). *Woman Between the Worlds: A Call to Your Ancestral and Indigenous Wisdom*. Hay House Publishers.

Daly, H. (2016). *Shadowy Beauty: The art of hypnopompic inquiry*. CIIS Doctoral Dissertation. UMI.

Deslauriers, D. (1992). *Dimensions of knowing: Narrative, Paradigm and Ritual*. ReVision, 14(4); 197-193.

Deslauriers, D. (2011). *Dreams at the boundary of Self and Others: Intersubjective fields, emotions and culture*. In S. Kakar (Ed). On dreams and dreaming. Penguin Viking.

Demos, E. V. (Ed). (1995) *Exploring affect. The selected writings of Silvan Tomkins*. NY: Cambridge University Press.

Domhoff, G.W. (1996). *Finding Meaning in Dreams a Quantitative Approach*. Springer.

Esser, T. (2013). *Lucid dreaming, Kundalini, the divine and nonduality: A transpersonal narrative study*. CIIS doctoral Dissertation. ProQuest Dissertations Publishing, 3560741. https://search.proquest.com/docview/1357147893

Ettinger, B. L. (2006). *The matrixial borderspace*. Minneapolis: University of Minnesota Press.

Ettinger, B. L. (2014). *Demeter-Persephone complex, entangled Aerials of the Psyche, and Sylvia Plath*. English Studies in Canada, 40(1), 123–154 doi: 10.1353/esc.2014.0010

Fordham, M. (1951). *The concept of the objective psyche*. Psychology and Psychotherapy, 24,4, 221–231 doi: 10.1111/j.2044-8341.1951.tb00407.x

Griffin, S. (1996). *The Eros in everyday life. Essays on ecology, gender and society*. Doubleday.

Hall, C. S. & Norby, V. J. (1972). *The individual and his dreams*. Signet.

Hall, J. A (1983). *Jungian dream interpretation. A handbook of theory and practice*. Inner City Books.

Hill, C. E. (2003). *Working with dreams in therapy: Facilitating exploration, insight, and action*. American Psychological Association.

Hillman, J. (1979). *The dream and the underworld*. Harper & Row.

Hillman, J. (1983). *Inter Views: Conversations with Laura Pozzo on psychotherapy, biography, love, soul, dreams, work, imagination and the state of culture*. Harper & Row.

Ingold, T. (2014). *That's enough about ethnography!* Hau: Journal of Ethnographic Theory, 4 (1): 383–395. doi: 10.14318/hau4.1.021

Jaenke, K. A. (2000). *Personal dreamscape as ancestral landscape*. [Doctoral dissertation, California Institute of Integral Studies]. UMI.

Jung, C.G. *The collected works*, Vol 7. Princeton, NJ: Princeton University Press.

Kaës, R, (2002). *The polyphonic texture of intersubjectivity in dreams*. In Neri, C., Pines, M., and Friedman, R. (eds) Dreams in Group Psychotherapy: Theory and Technique. 67-78. Jessica Kingsley.

Kahn, D., & Hobson, J. A. (2005). *Theory of mind in dreaming: Awareness of feelings and thoughts of others in dreams*. Dreaming, 15 (1), 48–57. doi: 10.1037/1053-0797.15.1.48

Kimmerer, R.W. (2013). *Braiding sweetgrass. Indigenous wisdom, scientific knowledge and the teachings of plants*. Milkweed Editions

Kuiken, D., Lee, M.N., Eng, T.C., & Singh, T. (2006). *The influence of impactful dreams on self-perceptual depth and spiritual transformation*. Dreaming, 16, 258-279. doi: 10.1037/1053-0797.16.4.258

Lippmann, P. (1998). *On the private and social nature of dreams*. Contemporary Psychoanalysis, 34 (2), 195-221. doi: 10.1080/00107530.1998.10746358

McNamara, P. (2004). *An Evolutionary Psychology of REM Sleep and Dreams*. Praeger Press.

Meltzer, D. (2009). *Dream life: A re-examination of the psychoanalytic theory and practice*. Karnac.

Merriam-Webster. Definition transsubjective. https://www.merriam-webster.com/dictionary/transsubjective. Retrieved Feb 5, 2019.

Nash, R. J. & Viray, S. (2014). *How stories heal: Writing our way to meaning & wholeness in the academy*. New York, NY: Peter Lang Publishing.

Novack, C.J. (1990). *Sharing the dance. Contact improvisation and American culture*. Madison, WI: University of Wisconsin Press.

Pfaff, D.W. (2015). *The altruistic brain*. NY: Oxford University Press.

Revonsuo, A., Tuominen, J. & Valli, K. (2015). *The Avatars in the Machine - Dreaming as a Simulation of Social Reality*. In T. Metzinger & J. M. Windt (Eds). Open MIND: 32. Frankfurt am Main: MIND Group. doi: 10.15502/9783958570375. https://open-mind.net/papers/the-avatars-in-the-machine-dreaming-as-a-simulation-of-social-reality/at-download/paper/pdf

Revonsuo, A. & Valli, K. (2000). *Dreaming and consciousness: Testing the threat simulation theory of the function of dreaming*. Psyche: An Interdisciplinary Journal of Research on Consciousness, 6(8). http://psycnet.apa.org/record/2001-03396-001

Stark-Smith, N. (2003). *A subjective history of Contact Improvisation*. In Ann Cooper Albright & David Gere (Eds). Taking by surprise. A dance improvisation reader (153-174). Middletown, CT: Wesleyan University Press.

Todorov, A., Fiske, S. & Prentice, D. (2011). *Social Neuroscience: Towards understanding the underpinnings of the social mind*. NY: Oxford University Press.

Teddlock, B. (2005). *The woman in the shaman's body. Reclaiming the feminine in religion and medicine*. Bantam.

Tomkins, S. (1982). *Affect, imagery, consciousness*. NY: Springer.

Whitney, A. (2017). *Map of the heart. An East-West understanding of heart intelligence and its application in counseling psychology*. CIIS Doctoral Dissertation. UMI.

Boundaries

They gave us coloring books

said use any of the crayons

but stay within the lines.

The borders held real still

against the chaos of blank space

against the lure of that freedom

our boundaries took their shape.

—*Meredith Sabini*

From ReVision Publishing

ETHNO Autobiography

Jürgen Werner Kremer
R Jackson-Paton

504 pages

Stories and Practices for
Unlearning Whiteness
Decolonization
Uncovering Ethnicities

Only $39.95
Includes shipping

Order from:
ReVision Publishing • PO Box 1855 • Sebastopol, CA 95473

from Vajra Publications

TRANSFORMATION OF CONSCIOUSNESS: POTENTIALS FOR OUR FUTURE

Dagmar Eigner & Jürgen Kremer (Eds.)

249 pages

Available from
Vajra Publications, Nepal
https://vajrabookshop.com/

VAJRA PUBLICATIONS

Available from
Amazon

$17.00

Transformation of Consciousness is an exploration of various approaches to impact our consciousness. The book points to potentials we as a species may need for our future survival.

Shamanic approaches are frequently viewed as premodern and thus mere historical remnants. The implication is that they are fascinating to help explain our past evolutionary history, but have little relevance for our future. When we disregard the significance of these ancient shamanic and Eastern paradigms, we disregard possible avenues to shift our thinking and our cultural practices for the benefit of our future survival.

Each author in this anthology discusses exit strategies out of the hall of mirrors that our contemporary world has created. Each contribution validates the importance of ancient traditions today, and the need for a more appropriate epistemology to describe consciousness processes.

Transformations of consciousness are needed not only to serve individual needs, but also to serve our general human need to know, understand, and make meaning. These transformations also support socio-cultural practices that are holistic, integrative, and balancing for individuals and communities.

www.ingramcontent.com/pod-product-compliance
Lightning Source LLC
Chambersburg PA
CBHW041637040426

42449CB00022B/3491